Banking and Insurance in the New China

ADVANCES IN CHINESE ECONOMIC STUDIES

Series Editor: Yanrui Wu, *Senior Lecturer in Economics, University of Western Australia, Australia*

The Chinese economy has been transformed dramatically in recent years. With its rapid economic growth and accession to the World Trade Organisation, China is emerging as an economic superpower. China's development experience provides valuable lessons to many countries in transition.

Advances in Chinese Economic Studies aims, as a series, to publish the best work on the Chinese economy by economists and other researchers throughout the world. It is intended to serve a wide readership including academics, students, business economists and other practitioners.

Titles in the series include:

The Evolution of the Stock Market in China's Transitional Economy
Chien-Hsun Chen and Hui-Tzu Shih

Financial Reform and Economic Development in China
James Laurenceson and Joseph C.H. Chai

China's Telecommunications Market
Entering a New Competitive Age
Ding Lu and Chee Kong Wong

Banking and Insurance in the New China
Competition and the Challenge of Accession to the WTO
Chien-Hsun Chen and Hui-Tzu Shih

Banking and Insurance in the New China

Competition and the Challenge of Accession to the WTO

Chien-Hsun Chen and Hui-Tzu Shih

Chung-Hua Institution for Economic Research, Taipei, Taiwan

ADVANCES IN CHINESE ECONOMIC STUDIES

Edward Elgar

Cheltenham, UK • Northampton, MA, USA

Published by
Edward Elgar Publishing Limited
Glensanda House
Montpellier Parade
Cheltenham
Glos GL50 1UA
UK

Edward Elgar Publishing, Inc.
136 West Street
Suite 202
Northampton
Massachusetts 01060
USA

A catalogue record for this book
is available from the British Library

Library of Congress Cataloguing in Publication Data

Chen, Chien-Hsun.
Banking and insurance in the new China: competition and the challenge of accession to the WTO/by Chien-Hsun Chen and Hui-Tzu Shih.
p. cm. — (Advances in Chinese economic studies)
Includes bibliographical references and index.
1. Banks and banking—China. 2. Insurance—China. 3. Competition—China. 4. World Trade Organization—China. I. Shih, Hui-Tzu. II. Title. III. Series.
HG3334.C452 2004
332.1'0951—dc22

2003061582

ISBN 1 84376 480 6

Printed and bound in Great Britain by MPG Books Ltd, Bodmin, Cornwall

Contents

Tables

Preface

The development of the knowledge economy has speeded up the process of financial globalization; competition in the financial sector therefore is no longer confined within national borders. As the motive power for economic growth, financial deepening can enhance the efficient allocation of societal resources, improving those channels linking investors to savers, making the allocation of capital more efficient, and reducing transaction and information costs. Although some progress has been made in reforming China's financial institutions, they are incapable of responding appropriately to both market forces and the increasing economic importance of the non-state sector.

On 11 December 2001, China successfully ended a fifteen-year long process of negotiation and joined the World Trade Organization (WTO). The landmark WTO accession indicated that China will continue to be a key player in the global economy and China will face an unprecedented challenge in the financial realm. Therefore, financial reform in itself has become a major concern to China's transitional economy, in particular, in the realm of banking and insurance.

The main theme of this book is to scrutinize the development and obstacle of China's banking and insurance industries during the process of institutional transformation, particularly the impact of China's WTO accession on these industries. With the unprecedented opening of China to the outside world in almost all sectors of the economy, the impacts of WTO accession on China will be immense. China's banking and insurance are now facing severe challenges as well as opportunities. The strength, weakness, opportunity and threat (SWOT) approach is undertaken to analyze the impact of WTO accession on the Chinese banking and insurance. The market structure–conduct–performance analytical framework (S–C–P) is also utilized to examine empirically the impact of market structure on operational performance management, and the impact of changes in market structure on managers' decision-making conduct for China's banking and insurance industries.

This book contains five chapters. Chapter 1 discusses the development and limitation of China's banking industry. During the process of institutional transformation, the reform of the financial system proceeded quite slowly, and the central planning element was still very noticeable. The transformation of the four big specialized state-owned banks into state-owned commercial banks did not really solve the problem of ownership rights. The role of private financial institutions was still very limited; the slow pace of development of private financial institutions prevented them from becoming an effective source of financing for the non-state sector. Although the state-owned commercial banks dominate the Chinese banking industry, they are affected by lack of clarity with respect to ownership and government interference. They lack effective risk management and incentive mechanisms, and their internal controls are weak. As a result, their operational performance has been poor, and they have been unable to compete effectively against the share-type commercial banks, whose operations are based on the market mechanism.

An excessively high non-performing loan ratio is a problem common to the whole of China's banking industry. Although there has been no large-scale bank failure in China, and no systemic payments crisis, individual banks have experienced crises, and there has been a systemic management crisis. This applies not only to the state-owned commercial banks, but also to the share-type commercial banks.

In order to solve the non-performing loan problem, in 1999, China established four asset management companies (AMCs). The biggest problem affecting AMCs' operation is the absence of a suitable market environment. State ownership of banks and enterprises means that new investors are still hobbled by old systems. The underdevelopment of China's financial markets and the lack of financial innovation restrict the methods that AMCs can use to dispose of assets. At the same time, the underdevelopment of intermediary institutions makes it difficult for AMCs to provide the necessary guidance services. Most investments in China are very conservative in their attitudes, and the level of transparency with respect to information is very low.

Chapter 2 analyzes the evolution of the Chinese insurance market. During the period of transformation of the economic system towards a market economy, as financial deepening has progressed 'insurance suppression' has gradually been eased. This process is known as 'insurance deepening'. Since the re-establishment of the Chinese insurance industry in 1979, as the economic system has been reformed and developed, insurance business has grown rapidly. China currently has 58 qualified insurance companies, of which 22 are foreign-owned life insurance companies and 16 are foreign-owned casualty insurance companies, compared with 20 domestic insurance companies; however, limitations on the scope of business and geographical area of operation have restricted the development of foreign-owned insurance companies in the China market.

The market concentration ratio and Herfindahl index calculations show the high extent to which the Chinese insurance market is monopolized by a handful of companies. Those companies operating nationwide account for a consistently high proportion of total premium income, while the market concentration level of the foreign insurance companies has never exceeded 1.29 percent. Although the market concentration level of those companies operating nationwide has been falling steadily, this indicates that their monopolization of the market is gradually weakening. Nevertheless, the Chinese insurance market is still dominated by these companies. Now that China is a member of the WTO, the restrictions on foreign-owned insurance companies' business areas and geographical area of operation will be relaxed, and the market share held by the foreign-owned insurance companies will gradually rise; this is likely to have a negative impact on the operational performance of the state-owned insurance companies

Chapter 3 evaluates the impact of the Chinese WTO accession of banking and insurance industries. The impact of WTO accession on the Chinese banking industry will be as follows: the market share of the Chinese banks will fall, the profitability of Chinese banks will be weakened, Chinese banks' liquidity will be reduced, WTO accession will make it difficult for banks to maintain normal operation, the policy banks will suffer most, the competition facing small and medium-sized commercial banks will become even fiercer, the difficulties of strengthening supervision to reduce risk and the difficulties of expanding macro-control over the financial sector will increase.

From the point of view of China's domestic banks, WTO accession is not without its advantages. It will help to improve the management capabilities of Chinese banks in the following ways. Since foreign banks possess huge quantities of funds and experience in the use of advanced management techniques, the entry of more foreign banks into the China market will encourage the introduction of the same kind of competitive mechanisms and rules as used in international markets. This will stimulate the development of the Chinese banking industry, helping to increase transparency with respect to lending, strengthen supervision, encourage the establishment of sound financial sector infrastructure, promote the modernization of financial systems and the establishment of the necessary legal framework, speed up the process of bank reform and improve the quality of service provided. It will also lead to a strengthening of international collaboration on supervision. The establishment of more channels for the inflow of foreign capital should ease the shortage of capital being experienced by China in the course of its economic development. Chinese banks will be able to establish branches overseas directly, helping them to develop overseas business and stake their place in the international financial markets.

Following WTO accession, as the internationalization of the financial sector continues, there will be challenges and opportunities for the Chinese insurance sector. The impact of WTO accession on China's insurance industry will be as follows: the market share held by the Chinese insurance companies is likely to fall, foreign insurance companies have a superior fund utilization capability, supervision of the insurance industry will get harder and the competition to secure talent will become even fiercer.

WTO accession will have the following benefits for the Chinese insurance market: it will stimulate the development of the Chinese insurance market, the number of different types of insurance product available will increase,

Chinese insurance companies will be able to develop international markets, WTO accession will help Chinese insurance companies to improve their management capabilities, it will stimulate the improvement of the regulatory mechanisms and China will have to set up its collaboration with regulators in other countries.

Chapter 4 examines empirically the relationship between market structure, behavior and performance in the Chinese banking and insurance industries. Regarding the banking sector, the period covered is 1995–2001; as this included the Asian financial crisis of 1997, the period has been divided into two sub-periods for comparison: 1995–1997 and 1998–2001. Since the sample is too small, the Spearman Rank Correlation is used for empirical testing.

The empirical results showed that, with the changes in the financial environment and the opening up of the capital markets, the business model adopted by China's banking industry has changed as well. For all Chinese banks, traditional deposit and loan business has increased as the market has expanded since the Asian financial crisis, causing average deposits per employee and average profits per employee to increase. Furthermore, as the size of their assets has increased, China's banks have started to pay more attention to customer service, increasing the number of employees; however, the increase in the number of employees has not been accompanied by an increase in professionalism, and no serious efforts have been made to develop new areas of business other than traditional deposit and loan business. Consequently, there has been no significant increase in earning ability.

Because of the near-oligopoly they enjoy, the state-owned commercial banks do remain strong, and they are spending a considerable amount on salaries, but the existence of moral hazard and the high cost of regulation mean that, even if an 'optimal contract' existed, it would not be sufficient to wholly eliminate expediency from manager conduct. As far as the number of employees is concerned, expense preference behavior can be seen; besides seeking to secure profits, managers may also display risk reduction and expense preference behavior.

The period covered for the insurance sector is 1998–2001, and the empirical findings indicate that as far as the Chinese insurance industry as a whole is concerned, as the market has expanded, insurance companies have begun to pay more attention to customer service in order to increase their market share. This has led them to increase the number of personnel; however, this increase in the number of employees has not been accompanied by an increase in professionalism. An increased premium income market share has led to an increased debt ratio; it can thus be seen that the Chinese insurance companies operating nationwide remain strong because of the near-monopoly they enjoy, and that they are spending a considerable amount on salaries. Owing to the restrictions imposed on foreign and joint venture insurance companies in terms of business areas and region of operation, their increased premium income market share has not helped them to increase their earning ability.

Chapter 5 focuses on the strategies can be adopted by the Chinese banking and insurance industries in response to the challenges presented by WTO accession and to prevent future financial crises. During this process of institutional transformation, the financial risk inherent in the old system and the risk created by institutional change exist side by side. With WTO accession and the opening up of the financial services industry to foreign companies, competition will become fiercer, leading to an increase in uncertainty, and thereby making the level of risk even greater.

The strategies that can be employed by Chinese banks in response to the challenges presented by WTO accession are as follows: clarification of property rights, promoting the adjustment of commercial banks' structure and the establishment of sound management mechanisms, eliminating the barriers between different segments of the financial services industry, development of traditional businesses combined with financial innovation, improving the quality of human resources, establishment of a market environment based on fair competition, speeding up the expansion of the market mechanism in the monetary policy tools, establishing a proper legal framework for the operations of foreign banks, providing a reasonable level of protection for state-owned commercial banks, gradual opening up of the financial markets, establishment of a legal system which conforms to international standards and increasing the level of transparency in the financial sector.

The strategies that can be utilized by the Chinese insurance industry in response to WTO accession are: speeding up of systemic reform in the insurance sector and the establishment of comprehensive management mechanisms, establishment of a comprehensive legal framework, promoting the establishment of sound intermediary institutions, establishing a fair competition environment, strengthening the regulations and cultivating insurance talent.

As the process of economic globalization has progressed, different kinds of production factors, and particularly capital, can flow rapidly all over the world. This globalization of the international flow of funds has stimulated competition within the global finance industry, leading to a deepening of financial liberalization in many countries. China, however, lacks a comprehensive, coherent legal framework for the protection of private property rights and regulation of economic activities. As a result, financial reform in China has been slow. The Chinese banking industry and insurance industry need to speed up the process of reform in line with the needs of globalization, and in response to the new circumstances following China's accession to the WTO. Some progress has been made, while much remains to be done; it will take time and careful consideration to get right the changes needed to make China's financial system more efficient.

Chien-Hsun Chen and Hui-Tzu Shih

1. China's Banking Industry during the Process of Institutional Transformation

1.1 THE DEVELOPMENT OF CHINA'S BANKING INDUSTRY

The development of the knowledge economy has speeded up the process of 'financial globalization', a term which refers to the collection, distribution, use and flow of funds on a global scale. The term includes international financial institutions and the exchange of different currencies between countries, but should also include the globalization of financial institutions, financial business and currencies. During this process of financial globalization, there has been a wave of mergers and acquisitions within the finance industry; existing banks have been encouraged to merge, to undertake transactional operations and to expand into new businesses, and as a result, competition within the financial sector is no longer confined within national borders. In order to adjust to this new type of competition and these new challenges, banks have been working to reorganize and re-engineer themselves, and indeed, since the early 1990s, bank re-engineering has become the core element of organizational reform, with an emphasis on being customer-oriented, the reform of traditional organizational structures and business processes, and a trend towards on-line banking and 'virtual banks'.

In terms of economic theory, opinion is divided as to whether the banking system can affect economic growth. Schumpeter (1934) for example, believed that if the banking system was working properly, then enterprises would be able to obtain their required financing, which would facilitate technological innovation and thus boost economic growth. Robinson (1952) held that it was the corporate sector which led the development of the financial sector; while Lucas (1988) also demonstrated a belief that economists had placed excessive emphasis on the role of the financial sector in economic growth. Levine (1997) used the function approach to analyze the relationship between the financial system and economic growth, suggesting that the emergence of financial markets helped to reduce transactions costs and information collection costs, making trade in both goods and services more convenient, encouraging saving, providing a form of administrative supervision with regard to company managers, helping to ensure the efficient distribution of resources, and spreading risk; thus, financial markets are thought to have helped to increase capital accumulation and boost economic growth.

As the motive power for economic growth, financial deepening can enhance the efficient allocation of societal resources, improving those channels linking investors to savers, making the allocation of capital more efficient and reducing transaction and information costs. McKinnon (1973) and Shaw (1973) believed that the efficient development of the financial system was beneficial to economic growth in developing nations, and that if the growth of the financial sector was obstructed, this would create an obstacle to economic development. This obstruction of the growth of the financial sector takes the form mainly of interest rate controls, bank lending policy and government interference in the normal operation of the market.

Endogenous growth theory describes the way in which sound financial organization along with the development of efficient financial intermediaries can improve the efficiency of capital allocation of capital and investment, thereby making capital more productive and contributing to economic growth (Bencivenga and Smith, 1991; Saint-Paul, 1992). The results of empirical research in the literature have shown that financial deepening has a positive impact on economic growth (Levine and Zervos, 1998; Rajan and Zingales, 1998; Levine et al., 2000; Cetorelli and Gambera, 2001), and that economic growth promotes financial deepening; indeed, that there is a feedback relationship between the two (Demetriades and Hussein, 1996).

During the period of institutional transformation in China, there have been two discernible stages in the financial deepening that has taken place. The first stage began with a shift from allocation to loans in the 1980s, and continued into the 1990s with transformation of the functions of the central bank and the commercialization of specialized state-owned banks. During this stage, banks became independent of the Ministry of Finance, and began to take on a financing role of their own; however, strict restrictions on new entrants meant that only four state-owned banks were involved in the provision of financing to state-owned enterprises (SOEs). The second stage began with the relaxation of restrictions on new entrants in 1993, following which, non-state-owned banks and non-bank financial institutions began to be established (Zheng and Gao, 2000).

In a classic centrally planned economy, money plays only an intermediary role in transactions, and the financial system consists of one national bank and its branches, constituting a 'monobank'. Combined within the national bank are the functions of both central bank and commercial bank, and within this system, all financial behavior between households, and between households and enterprises, involves payment in cash, while transactions between SOEs are handled by book entry.

Prior to the economic reforms which began in 1979, China had a highly centralized, highly unified financial system which was the product of a command economy. Cash was printed on command, as decided by the central planning agencies, while the People's Bank of China (PBC) issued cash as instructed by the central government; which, in turn, determined how much cash would be issued by its branches at the provincial, municipal and autonomous regional level. Control over the allocation of credit was also highly centralized. The funds which SOEs required for fixed asset investment and to meet the bulk of their working capital needs were provided free of charge by the Ministry of Finance, with the PBC being responsible only for providing additional working capital and loans; bank credit was thus used to meet only seasonal and extraordinary funding needs (Huang, 1992). The provision of 'no-cost' funding meant that SOEs were subject only to soft budget constraints, and as a result, their managerial performance was poor (Kornai, 1980).

Prior to the economic reforms, the main characteristics of the financial system were as follows: (i) financial operation and management were highly centralized and came under the direction of the government; (ii) the PBC acted as the center for cash, credit and settlement, functioning as a national bank; (iii) the main function of banks was merely one of adjustment; and (iv) the PBC had a planning function, serving as the executive, supervisory and accounting agency for the entire planned economy.

During the subsequent process of institutional transformation, the command economy was gradually replaced by a guided planned economy. Whereas in the past agricultural loans, the purchase of agricultural products and the allocation of cash within villages had all been handled at the level of the commune or production brigade, with the implementation of the household responsibility system the earlier system had to be changed, resulting in the household becoming the basic unit. With the adjustment of the prices paid for agricultural products, the establishment of township and village enterprises (TVEs), the granting of greater autonomy to enterprises, an increase in the proportion of profits that could be retained, and the reform of the wage system, the incomes of both urban and rural residents rose. As a result, the amount of money being deposited in the bank increased, and with more money coming in, the bank was in a position to increase its lending.

The promulgation, on 23 February 1979, of the State Council Notification Regarding the Re-establishment of the Agricultural Bank of China, led to the re-establishment of the Agricultural Bank of China, with responsibility for cash management and loan business within rural communities. On 13 March the same year, the Bank of China was spun off from the PBC to be responsible for foreign exchange business. This was followed by the establishment of the Industrial and Commercial Bank of China in April 1984 and the People's Construction Bank of China in November 1985.

The Industrial and Commercial Bank of China subsequently assumed responsibility for all commercial banking, the Agricultural Bank of China for agricultural lending, the Bank of China for foreign exchange business, and the People's Construction Bank of China for project finance.

In 1983, the State Council issued the Decision Regarding the Limiting of the People's Bank of China to the Function of Central Bank, which meant that the PBC would no longer handle deposit and loan business, and would instead be involved mainly in the setting of monetary policy in order to exercise overall direction over the economy. Besides commercial banking business, the state-owned specialized banks would also provide policy loans (non-profit making). For example, with regard to the purchase of agricultural products, the banks were all too well aware that the companies involved in grain purchase were making a loss, but they were still required to provide them with loans. As a result, the banks' bad debt ratio mounted. At the same time, the small margin between loans and deposit interest rates meant that banks' profits were reduced, and in some cases, they found themselves making a loss. Policy loans have accounted for approximately one third of total loans since 1990; however, in 1994, with the establishment of development banks, all policy loan business was divested, and the specialized state-owned banks were transformed into commercial banks with proper asset liability ratio management and an effort to improve risk management.

The Commercial Banking Law of 1995 stipulated that commercial banks must be established as corporate persons in accordance with Company Law. The minimum registered capital of state-owned commercial banks and share-type (shareholding) commercial banks was set at renminbi (RMB) 1 billion. Senior managers had to have at least a university degree in finance, and eight years' experience in the financial sector (ten years in the case of state-owned commercial banks). At least 60 percent of bank employees had to either have previous experience in the financial sector or have a degree in finance from a university or junior college. Where a share-type commercial bank established a branch, the head office was required to allocate at least RMB100 million for working capital, while the total amount allocated to all branches was not permitted to exceed 60 percent of the bank's total capital. In the case of branches established outside urban areas, the amount of working capital allocated had to be at least RMB50 million, while the registered capital of city banks had to be at least RMB100 million. Senior managers of city banks were also required to have at least a degree in finance, and eight years' experience in the financial sector. At least 60 percent of city bank employees had to either have previous experience in the financial sector or have a degree in finance from a university or junior college. City banks were mainly formed by the reorganization of urban credit cooperatives, and their organization had only two levels, head office and branch. Branches outside urban areas were to be established by the reorganization of existing credit cooperatives.

During the process of institutional transformation, the reform of the financial system proceeded very slowly, and the central planning element was still very much in evidence. The transformation of the four big specialized state-owned banks into state-owned commercial banks did not really solve the problem of ownership rights and the role of private financial institutions was still very limited. The slow pace of development of private financial institutions prevented them from becoming an effective source of financing for the non-state sector. Financial education was still focused very much on Chinese financial practice, being divorced from the mainstream of international financial business. As a result, there was a severe shortage of people with in-depth knowledge of derivatives, financial regulation and international practice, creating an obstacle to financial deepening and financial innovation (Cao, 2000; Pan, 2001).

As a result of the process of financial system transformation, the main elements of China's financial system took on the following form: (i) the PBC was the central bank; (ii) the policy banks (or development banks) included the State Development Bank, Export–Import Bank and Agriculture Development Bank; (iii) the state-owned commercial banks included the Industrial and Commercial Bank of China, the Agricultural Bank of China, the Bank of China and the China Construction Bank; (iv) the share-type commercial banks included national commercial banks such as the Bank of Communication, CITIC Industrial Bank, China Everbright Bank, Hua Xia Bank, China Minsheng Bank, Guangdong Development Bank, Shenzhen Development Bank, China Merchants Bank and Fujian Development Bank, along with regional banks such as the housing savings banks (the Yantai Housing Savings Bank and Bengbu Housing Savings Bank), city banks and foreign banks; and (v) non-bank financial institutions included insurance companies, trust and investment companies, securities firms, finance companies and credit cooperatives.

By the end of 2000, the four big state-owned commercial banks had total assets (both inside and outside China) of RMB12,362.13 billion, growing at an annual rate of 8.3 percent. Outstanding loans totalled RMB6,690.13 billion, with deposits totalling RMB9,334.09 billion, growing at an annual rate of 9.1 percent (*Almanac of China's Finance and Banking*, 2001). Since all property belongs to the people, there is a 'virtual' property rights system, operating very differently from a market economy, with the main defects of the system being as follows: (i) since the state-owned banks are closely connected with the government; the banks end up becoming a tool for the implementation of economic policy; (ii) the similarity between state-owned banks and SOEs with respect to property rights has resulted in the operating risk of SOEs being transferred to the state-owned banks on a large scale, creating systemic financial risk; (iii) the state-owned banks still have to perform policy tasks; for example, the Industrial and Commercial Bank of China has to provide loans to loss-making SOEs, and the Agricultural Bank of China has to provide loans to impoverished regions and comprehensive agricultural development loans; (iv) under the state-ownership system, the state-owned commercial banks are organized as Category One juristic persons. The head office is the legal representative, and the calculator and distributor of profits, while the institution to which it belongs is not in a legal sense an owner, nor does it have the legal status of economic entity, thus creating a situation where property rights relationships within the banking system are very unclear, such that it is impossible to create an effective incentive mechanism, or establish a proper corporate governance structure; and (v) the problem of moral hazard is widespread, making it very difficult to control operating risks.

Under the traditional planned economy system, SOEs were dependent on the Ministry of Finance for their funding, but since the economic reforms began, there has been a gradual shift towards reliance on bank loans. The operational performance of most SOEs is, however, very poor, making it impossible for them to repay the huge loans given to them by the state-owned banks. As a result, all the banks have amassed huge amounts of non-performing loans, and the government has had to intervene actively in the disposal of these non-performing assets, which has had a serious negative impact on innovation in the state-owned commercial banking sector. The low efficiency of state-owned banks has reduced the efficiency with which savings can be converted into investment, and has prevented many companies with considerable potential from securing access to financing, thereby making it more difficult for China to maintain its high economic growth rate. At the same time, all the state-owned banks still have many inefficient, loss-making branches, seriously undermining any efforts they make to improve their operational performance. Other problems include the non-existence of boards of directors, structural weaknesses, excessively large, over-complicated organizational systems, the fact that managers are appointed by the government, the absence of a performance auditing system at both the decision-making and executive level, and low transparency in management (Li, Guofeng, 2001; Huang, 2002).

China's policy banks were all established by the government as a means of implementing industrial policy and achieve the goals of regional development. Their main sources of funding are allocations from the government, the issuing of bank debentures, loans from the PBC, and so on.

These banks do not take deposits from the public, and the maximization of profit is not their main operational objective. The State Development Bank was established on 17 March 1994, with its main task being to provide funding for key national development projects. The Bank's head office has registered capital of RMB50 billion and is located in Beijing, with the first of its branches being established in Wuhan in 1996. The Export–Import Bank was established on 1 July 1994 to provide export loans, guarantees, and so on, with registered capital of RMB3.38 billion, all of which was provided by the government. Although it does have a head office in Beijing, it nevertheless has no operational branches. The Agricultural Development Bank was established on 18 November 1994 with registered capital of RMB20 billion, a head office, again located in Beijing and has branches all over China. The Agricultural Development Bank is mainly involved in providing loans for the storage and purchase of important agricultural products such as grain, cotton and oil, as well as providing comprehensive agricultural development loans, loans to impoverished regions, and loans for irrigation and technology upgrading projects.

At the end of 2000, the State Development Bank had total assets of RMB808.3 billion, demonstrating an annual rate of 17.8 percent, total liabilities of RMB754.3 billion, growing at an annual rate of 18.8 percent, and total outstanding loans of RMB179.6 billion (of which RMB36.9 billion were for key national construction projects, accounting for 89 percent of the total loans provided for such projects). In the same year, the Export–Import Bank had total assets of RMB68.26 billion, total liabilities of RMB62.858 billion, and total outstanding loans of RMB34.575 billion (growing at an annual rate of 22.9 percent). It had provided export loan guarantees worth US$1.234 billion and external guarantees worth US$2.32 billion (*Almanac of China's Finance and Banking*, 2001).

The share-type commercial banks are new banks which developed outside the existing state-owned bank system. These banks can be divided into two development models, of a policy-oriented and a market-oriented nature. The policy-oriented model is that displayed by share-type banks which took shape within the restrictions imposed by government policy; these banks have a clear advantage in terms of access to government resources and are characterized by a high level of government interference in their operations. Examples include the Shenzhen Development Bank, Guangdong Development Bank, Fujian Development Bank, Shanghai Pudong Development Bank and Hainan Development Bank (which folded in June 1998). These banks were established by local governments as a means of providing funding for the Special Economic Zones (SEZs), promoting local economic development and breaking the monopoly previously held by the state-owned banks. Their equity structure is clear, they have clear operational positioning, and they enjoy a close relationship with local government. The Yantai Housing Savings Bank and Bengbu Housing Savings Bank were established in the mid-1980s in line with Chinese government housing policy, in order to promote the development of the housing industry.

The market-oriented development model is that displayed by those banks established in accordance with the needs of economic development, at the volition of the investors, and in accordance with proper legal procedures. These banks display more autonomy in their operations; the bulk of them are city banks established by the conversion of existing urban credit cooperatives.

Most of the new commercial banks were established as share companies, in accordance with the provisions of Company Law, with these share-type commercial banks being much more able to establish modern governance mechanisms. By the end of 2000, China had 110 share-type commercial banks, with total assets of RMB2.56 trillion, accounting for 19 percent of the assets of China's financial system as a whole (RMB13.7 trillion). Trans-regional and national share-type commercial banks include China Merchants Bank, CITIC Industrial Bank, China Everbright Bank, Hua Xia Bank, Bank of Communication, China Minsheng Bank, Guangdong Development Bank, Shenzhen Development Bank, Shanghai Pudong Development Bank and Fujian Development Bank. At the end of 2000, these ten banks had total assets of RMB1.8525 trillion, accounting for 13.52 percent of the total assets in China's financial system. There were 99 city banks, with total assets of RMB709.6 billion, accounting for a further 5.18 percent of the Chinese financial system's total assets. There were also 177 foreign banks operating in China, with total assets of US$34.6 billion, accounting for approximately 2.09 percent of all assets within China's financial system (Deng, 2001). Three share-type commercial banks – Shenzhen Development Bank, Shanghai Pudong Development Bank and China Minsheng Bank – were listed on the stock exchange. Furthermore, the first mergers and reorganizations in China's banking industry have already taken place among the share-type banks; in 1996, for example, Guangdong Development Bank acquired Zhongyin Trust and Investment Company, and in March 1999, China Everbright Bank acquired 137 branches (from 29 regional branches) from China Investment Bank.

Ever since the Asian financial crisis of 1997, China has been actively working to speed up the pace of financial reform in order to prevent the occurrence of a similar crisis in the future. Some of the most important measures adopted are as follows (Jiao, 2000; Li and Li, 2001).

1. *Improving overall financial control*: On 1 January 1998, the Chinese government abolished the loan quotas which had previously applied to

state-owned commercial banks, and began the promotion of asset liability ratio management and risk control. The PBC no longer gave instructions as to how loans should be allocated in each quarter and year; and instead, provided only guidance. In March 1998, each financial institution's time deposit reserve account and prepared deposit account were merged into a reserve account. The interest rate on the deposit reserve was reduced from 13 percent to 8 percent, and further still to 6 percent in November 1999. Since June 1996, interest rates have been reduced several times, with efforts being made to have interest rates determined by the market. The main goal here is to increase the margin by which interest rates on RMB loans can float. For example, on 31 October 1998, the PBC increased the margin by which interest rates on loans to small businesses were allowed to float; the maximum rate of increase on loans to small businesses by commercial banks and city credit cooperatives was increased from 10 percent to 20 percent, while the maximum rate of increase on loans by rural credit cooperatives was increased from 40 percent to 50 percent.

On 21 September 2000, the foreign currency interest management system was overhauled, with reforms which included the relaxation of restrictions on foreign currency loan interest rates. For deposits of US$3 million (or the equivalent in other currencies) or higher, the interest rate could now be set by negotiation between the financial institution and their customer; for smaller deposits the rate would be set by negotiation within the banking industry. The PBC also decided that as from 21 February 2002, the interest rate on RMB deposits and loans and other annual interest rates on deposits would be reduced, by an average of 0.25 percent. The interest rate on current deposits would be reduced by 0.27 percentage points from 0.99 percent to 0.72 percent, while the interest rate on one-year time deposit accounts would also be reduced by 0.27 percent, from 2.25 percent to 1.98 percent. Interest rates on loans would be reduced by an average of 0.5 percent. The interest rate on six-month loans being reduced by 0.54 percent, from 5.58 percent to 5.04 percent, and was also reduced by 0.54 percent on one-year loans, from 5.85 percent to 5.31 percent (*Guoji Jinrong Bao*, 21 February 2002).

2. *Strengthening of financial supervision*: During the mid-1980s, as the pace of institutional transformation and financial reform speeded up, the market mechanism was introduced into the financial sector. The boundaries between the business areas of the different specialized banks were gradually blurred, and competition became increasingly fierce. A large number of non-financial institutions moved into the financial markets, including trust and investment companies, securities firms, leasing companies, urban and rural credit cooperatives and insurance companies. Given that competition in their original areas of business was extremely fierce, and owing also to the lack of

effective supervision, non-bank financial institutions began moving into the banking business, while banks expanded into the trust, securities, investment and insurance businesses. Not only did this increase the level of operational risk for banks, it also contributed to the growth of a bubble economy, making overall supervision of the financial sector more difficult; and, eventually, the existing regulatory system was hardly able to operate at all. In 1998, the government introduced a system aimed at separating the banking, securities and insurance industries, with the simultaneous introduction of separate supervisory systems. The PBC was no longer responsible for supervision of the securities and insurance industries; supervision of the former was transferred to the China Securities Regulatory Commission (CSRC), while supervision of the latter became the responsibility of the China Insurance Regulatory Commission (CIRC).

In order to increase the independence of the PBC and strengthen its supervisory and regulatory capabilities, in 1998 the supervisory functions of its provincial branches were eliminated, and nine trans-provincial branches were established based on zones of economic activity. These were based in Tianjin, Shenyang, Shanghai, Nanjing, Jinan, Wuhan, Guangzhou, Chengdu and Xian to oversee financial business as well as the financial institutions within these regions. In 1999 a financial supervisory system of responsibility was established, delineating the responsibilities of head offices and branches (Hong, 2001).

In April 2000, the State Council announced the implementation of a system whereby bank customers would have to use their real name when opening an account, while also requiring financial institutions to maintain confidentiality with respect to their depositors' accounts, in order to ensure that depositors' rights were protected. In 2001, the PBC issued the Notification Regarding Problems Relating to the Management of Personal Housing Loans and Notification Regarding the Prohibition of Personal Consumer Loans for Non-specified Purposes. These regulations required commercial banks to undertake strict auditing of housing loans, and prohibited the granting of consumer loans for non-specific purposes. In 2002, the main focus of bank supervision work in China was placed upon strengthening the supervision of financial institutions and other juristic persons, reducing the quantity of non-performing loans and raising profit levels.

In 2002, China adopted a series of measures to further strengthen financial supervision and management to oversee banks and to reduce potential financial risk. Since the operation of underground banks is closely related to money laundering, illegal foreign exchange transactions and currency smuggling, China has been intensifying its effort to combat illegal dealing in foreign exchange, to rectify the order of foreign exchange trading; for example, on 28 and 29 August 2002, Guandong cracked down on eleven underground banks in Guangzhou, Zhuhai, Foshan, Dongguan and Shunde. Most of them operated illegal trading of foreign currencies and were jointly run by local investors and Hong Kong, Macao and Taiwan partners. The PBC was also to set up a department to detect money laundering and to cut off funds for terrorist organizations as well as stem tax evasion and corruption. Moreover, China's first anti-money laundering regulation came into effect on 1 March 2003 (*China Daily*, 14 January 2003).

To maintain financial stability, on 28 November 2002, the PBC asked commercial banks to stop 'irregular' practices in pursuit of larger market share which may undermine the financial stability, such as raising interest rates on deposits, paying fees and giving gifts to depositors. 'Irregular' practices are more common among smaller banks, since they have small clients and outlets to collect deposits. One key area that draws the PBC's attention is the emerging problems in the real estate sector. To avoid a potential financial crisis in the sector, the PBC had undertaken, since June 2001, measures to curb malpractices such as the lowering of down payment for property purchases without proper authorization, granting of loans without necessary certification and diverting of working capital to real estate projects. The new regulation requires developers to have funds equal to at least 30 percent of the cost of the project they are planning. Individual housing buyers can borrow no more than 60 percent of the house price (*Xinhua News Agency*, 5 December 2002). In December 2002, the Central Economic Working Conference proposed to set up a China Banking Regulatory Commission to strengthen financial supervision.

3. *Active promotion of commercial banks reform*: Since commercial banks are an important element in the implementation of monetary policy; the Chinese government needs to speed up the reform of its state-owned commercial bank ownership rights in order to create a better governance mechanism. This includes the strengthening of juristic person management, strengthening of internal controls, the establishment of auditing and supervisory systems which are relatively independent (but also supervised directly by the head office), creation of a sound asset and liability management system, separation of responsibility for loan granting and loan review, the establishment of a proper loan guarantee system, and a credit quality management responsibility system, and so on.

The government needs to assign supervisors to each of the fifteen key financial institutions, stepping up the supervision of state-owned financial institutions, and to promote stock market listing of share-type commercial banks, in order to improve their capital adequacy ratios and upgrade their corporate governance mechanisms (an example here is the listing of China

Minsheng Bank in November 2000). The government has revised its method for writing off non-performing loans of commercial banks, shifting over from a system where the amount of non-performing loans is calculated at the beginning of the year to a system whereby an amount equivalent to 1 percent of the total outstanding loan balance is allocated to a non-performing loan reserve at the end of each year, with an additional bad debt reserve equivalent to 3 percent of accounts receivable at year end, making it easier for commercial banks to write off their non-performing assets.

In addition, with regard to market entry, operation and market exit, the PBC can now make use of a variety of methods (including the injection of capital, conversion of debt to equity, mergers, closure and bankruptcy) to deal with troubled financial institutions, thereby preventing financial crises. On 24 April 2002, the PBC promulgated the Notification Regarding Problems Relating to the Management of the Entry of New Chinese Commercial Banks into the Market; this required all state-owned banks and share-type commercial banks to gradually reduce the number of different levels of branches, and upgrade their branches' function. It was made a strict requirement that commercial banks should aim to establish an organization based on a head office, regional branches, local branches, streamlining their branch structure, and establishing and adjusting branches in line with the needs of economic development and the market, including making the best use of their own management and control capabilities. In principle, the PBC would no longer accept applications for the establishment of branches at lower than local branch level and, given that the total number of commercial bank branches was too high while average assets per employee were too low and regional distribution was inappropriate, regulations were established to allow banks to adjust their branch structure within the same city, or between different cities (at the same level) in the same province (*Zhonghua Gongshang Shibao*, 25 April 2002).

Market Structure in the Banking Industry

In this section, the concentration ratio (CRn) and the Herfindahl index (Scherer, 1980) are applied to examine China's banking industry's deposits, loans, assets and net profit, using the data provided on *Zhong Jing Wang* and in the *Almanac of China's Finance and Banking* for the years 1997–2002 to measure the level of market concentration in China's banking industry.

$$CRn = \sum_{i=1}^{n}(S_i) = \sum_{i=1}^{n} X_i \Big/ \sum_{i=1}^{m} X_i \qquad (1.1)$$

where n represents the number of banks and m represents the total number of banks and

$$H = \sum_{i=1}^{n} (X_i / T)^2 \qquad (1.2)$$

where n represents the number of banks and T represents total market scale.

For the purposes of comparative analysis, the banking industry is divided into three main categories, policy banks, state-owned commercial banks and share-type banks, with the estimation results being provided in Tables 1.1 and 1.2.

The results of calculation using CRn and the Herfindahl index show that the level of concentration among existing state-owned commercial banks in terms of deposits, loans, assets and net profits displays a high level of oligopolization. This is largely due to the high degree of protection provided by the government to state-owned banks. In the case of loan business, for example, the PBC allows only the four big state-owned commercial banks to undertake car purchase and consumer loan business (launched in 1995), housing loans, long-term loans for basic construction, and so on; share-type banks are excluded from these areas of businesses.

All interest rates on deposits are set by the PBC in accordance with the provisions of the Banking Law. As a result, the market mechanism does not operate with respect to deposit rates, and has been replaced by competition which is not based on price, where the only way to secure more deposits is to establish more branches. The state-owned commercial banks have an advantage here too. However, while the state-owned commercial banks are maintaining their share of deposits, their share of total loans, assets and net profits is gradually falling, which shows that their dominance of the market is being reduced. The new share-type commercial banks provide financing to small and medium enterprises (SMEs) which have lower credit ratings, are smaller, and find it difficult to secure financing from the state-owned commercial banks.[1] As a result, the share-type commercial banks are able to compete against the state-owned commercial banks. During the period 1997–1998, the share-type commercial banks had a higher concentration in terms of net profits than the state-owned commercial banks, which shows that during this period the share-type commercial banks were significantly more competitive than the state-owned commercial banks.

Table 1.1 CR Indices for China's Banking Market, 1994–2001 (%)

		1994	1995	1996	1997
Deposits	CRd for policy banks	0.01	0.55	0.57	0.57
	CRd for state-owned commercial banks	**81.58**	**77.49**	**76.87**	**73.90**
	CRd for share-type commercial banks	8.93	9.11	9.44	9.76
Loans	CRl for policy banks	1.95	12.10	13.65	15.94
	CRl for state-owned commercial banks	**74.60**	**73.27**	**71.64**	**67.22**
	CRl for share-type commercial banks	5.63	5.82	6.19	6.00
Assets	CRa for policy banks	1.95	6.14	6.65	7.20
	CRa for state-owned commercial banks	**74.60**	**66.20**	**57.41**	**45.41**
	CRa for share-type commercial banks	5.63	5.29	5.56	5.67
Net Profits	CRp for policy banks	–3.44	0.98	4.37	–4.99
	CRp for state-owned commercial banks	**50.57**	**69.23**	**57.39**	37.37
	CRp for share-type commercial banks	**52.19**	29.46	37.22	**65.94**
		1998	**1999**	**2000**	**2001**
Deposits	CRd for policy banks	0.21	0.34	0.60	0.58
	CRd for state-owned commercial banks	**74.27**	**73.86**	**72.76**	**67.79**
	CRd for share-type commercial banks	9.64	7.58	8.84	11.13
Loans	CRl for policy banks	10.62	10.37	12.53	12.51
	CRl for state-owned commercial banks	**66.17**	**49.31**	**45.07**	**46.29**
	CRl for share-type commercial banks	5.98	6.24	7.28	8.40
Assets	CRa for policy banks	6.49	6.26	6.42	5.45
	CRa for state-owned commercial banks	**45.10**	**43.20**	**45.13**	**37.65**
	CRa for share-type commercial banks	5.51	5.91	7.50	7.39
Net Profits	CRp for policy banks	7.09	5.79	9.64	12.10
	CRp for state-owned commercial banks	37.73	**71.83**	**68.74**	**59.38**
	CRp for share-type commercial banks	**53.67**	21.76	20.43	28.52

Source: Compiled for this research.

Table 1.2 Herfindahl Indices for China's Banking Market, 1994–2001 (%)

		1995	1996	1997	1998
Deposits	Hd for policy banks	0.0026	0.0032	0.0031	0.0004
	Hd for state-owned commercial banks	**16.34**	**15.84**	**14.74**	**14.88**
	Hd for share-type commercial banks	0.27	0.25	0.23	0.20
Loans	Hl for policy banks	0.87	1.05	1.42	0.52
	Hl for state-owned commercial banks	**14.75**	**13.99**	**12.29**	**11.71**
	Hl for share-type commercial banks	0.11	0.11	0.10	0.09
Assets	Ha for policy banks	0.22	0.25	0.29	0.21
	Ha for state-owned commercial banks	**12.24**	**9.52**	**5.49**	**5.32**
	Ha for share-type commercial banks	0.09	0.08	0.07	0.07
Net Profits	Hp for policy banks	0.00	0.12	1.39	0.25
	Hp for state-owned commercial banks	**13.70**	**13.27**	**7.40**	**6.35**
	Hp for share-type commercial banks	2.72	3.36	**8.49**	4.23

		1999	2000	2001
Deposits	Hd for policy banks	0.0006	0.0018	0.0000003
	Hd for state-owned commercial banks	**14.72**	**14.11**	**12.39**
	Hd for share-type commercial banks	0.12	0.12	0.16
Loans	Hl for policy banks	0.52	0.73	0.72
	Hl for state-owned commercial banks	**8.81**	**7.24**	**7.64**
	Hl for share-type commercial banks	0.09	0.10	0.10
Assets	Ha for policy banks	0.18	0.19	0.14
	Ha for state-owned commercial banks	**4.85**	**5.37**	**3.73**
	Ha for share-type commercial banks	0.07	0.09	0.08
Net Profits	Hp for policy banks	0.15	0.43	0.92
	Hp for state-owned commercial banks	**23.19**	**18.76**	**15.41**
	Hp for share-type commercial banks	0.78	0.69	1.10

Source: Compiled for this research.

Human Resources Structure in the Banking Industry

An examination of the age structure of the banking industry shows that, for policy banks, state-owned commercial banks and share-type commercial banks, the majority of employees are aged 40 or under. However, in the policy banks the proportion of employees aged 55 or over is noticeably higher than in the state-owned commercial banks and share-type commercial banks; this may be related to the fact that personnel appointments in the policy banks are more closely controlled by the government (see Table 1.3).

Table 1.3 The Age Structure of China's Banking Industry, 1998–2001 (%)

	2001							
	Under 30	31–35	36–40	41–45	46–50	51–54	55–59	60–
Policy banks	**17.63**	13.90	**30.22**	**22.32**	8.55	3.97	3.29	0.11
State-owned commercial banks	**25.14**	**27.04**	**24.99**	12.22	6.81	2.34	1.44	0.02
Share-type commercial banks	**46.90**	**17.56**	**19.70**	6.49	6.59	1.91	0.81	0.02
	2000							
	Under 30	31–35	36–40	41–45	46–50	51–54	55–59	60–
Policy banks	21.61	**17.65**	**27.16**	**17.13**	8.29	4.51	3.60	0.05
State-owned commercial banks	**36.36**	**20.21**	**22.21**	15.29	5.48	1.84	0.80	0.02
Share-type commercial banks	**51.27**	**15.27**	**18.38**	6.57	6.05	1.65	0.80	0.02
	1999							
	Under 30	31–35	36–40	41–45	46–50	51–54	55–59	60–
Policy banks	**23.27**	**20.09**	**25.43**	16.19	7.31	4.25	3.43	0.04
State-owned commercial banks	**45.72**	**16.43**	13.80	15.54	5.22	2.10	1.19	0.01
Share-type commercial banks	**54.75**	**13.67**	**16.69**	6.96	5.65	1.63	0.64	0.02
	1998							
	Under 30	31–35	36–40	41–45	46–50	51–54	55–59	60–
Policy banks	**23.55**	**23.78**	**23.27**	14.83	6.92	4.33	3.28	0.03
State-owned commercial banks	**38.24**	**21.37**	**18.76**	11.64	5.85	2.41	1.06	0.68
Share-type commercial banks	**58.31**	**14.01**	**13.89**	6.94	4.86	1.31	0.65	0.03

Source: Compiled for this research.

As regards the educational level structure, for policy banks, state-owned commercial banks and share-type commercial banks, the bulk of employees are graduates of junior colleges, technical secondary schools or senior high schools. Share-type commercial banks have a markedly higher proportion of university graduates than policy banks and state-owned commercial banks, while policy banks and state-owned commercial banks have a higher proportion of employees educated to junior high school level or below. This is related to the fact that the share-type commercial banks have better governance mechanisms, and are able to offer high salaries to attract high-quality personnel; as a result, their personnel are of a higher caliber (see Table 1.4).

Table 1.4 The Educational Level Structure of China's Banking Industry, 1998–2001 (%)

				2001			
	PhD	Masters	University	Junior College	Technical Secondary	Senior High	Junior High or lower
Policy banks	0.08	1.37	16.97	**38.12**	**20.04**	**17.34**	6.08
State-owned commercial banks	0.02	0.60	13.89	**37.58**	**21.75**	**21.82**	4.34
Share-type commercial banks	0.10	3.18	**28.16**	**41.77**	**14.56**	9.96	2.28
				2000			
	PhD	Masters	University	Junior College	Technical Secondary	Senior High	Junior High or lower
Policy banks	0.08	1.55	16.31	**35.80**	**20.48**	**18.40**	7.37
State-owned commercial banks	0.01	0.39	12.42	**36.35**	**22.80**	**22.30**	5.73
Share-type commercial banks	0.08	2.84	**25.13**	**41.19**	**15.62**	12.81	2.33
				1999			
	PhD	Masters	University	Junior College	Technical Secondary	Senior High	Junior High or lower
Policy banks	0.08	1.34	14.23	34.01	22.32	20.05	7.97
State-owned commercial banks	0.00	0.52	11.48	**32.03**	**24.40**	**23.67**	7.91
Share-type commercial banks	0.04	2.18	**21.43**	**40.72**	**19.78**	12.97	2.88

Table 1.4 Continued

	1998						
	PhD	Masters	University	Junior College	Technical Secondary	Senior High	Junior High or lower
Policy banks	0.07	0.88	11.49	**32.95**	**23.68**	**22.06**	8.87
State-owned commercial banks	0.01	0.38	9.24	**30.27**	**25.43**	**26.90**	7.77
Share-type commercial banks	0.07	1.94	**19.62**	**39.22**	**19.38**	16.20	3.58

Source: Compiled for this research.

With regard to the personnel structure of China's banks, as can be seen from Table 1.5 this is a classic pyramid-type structure, although the proportion of high-ranking personnel is noticeably higher in the policy banks. Having an advantage in human resources is the key to success in the banking industry; therefore, in order to upgrade the overall competitiveness of China's banking industry; the quality of the industry's human resources will need to be improved.

Table 1.5 Personnel Structure of China's Banking Industry, 1998–2001 (%)

	2001		
	Senior	Intermediate	Junior
Policy banks	5.14	38.51	**56.35**
State-owned commercial banks	1.55	29.06	**69.39**
Share-type commercial banks	3.01	40.80	**56.19**
	2000		
	Senior	Intermediate	Junior
Policy banks	4.82	37.95	**57.23**
State-owned commercial banks	1.40	27.24	**71.37**
Share-type commercial banks	2.68	37.53	**59.79**
	1999		
	Senior	Intermediate	Junior
Policy banks	4.66	36.94	**58.40**
State-owned commercial banks	1.57	26.12	**72.31**
Share-type commercial banks	2.43	34.82	**62.75**

Table 1.5 Continued

	1998		
	Senior	Intermediate	Junior
Policy banks	4.45	35.22	**60.34**
State-owned commercial banks	1.44	24.40	**74.16**
Share-type commercial banks	2.40	32.27	**65.33**

Source: Compiled for this research.

Operational Performance in the Banking Industry

In order to analyze the operational performance of the banking industry, this study uses return on assets (ROA), net profit rate and return on capital.

$$\text{ROA} = \text{Net profit before tax/Total assets} * 100\% \qquad (1.3)$$

$$\text{Net profit rate} = \text{Net profit before tax/operating revenue} * 100\% \qquad (1.4)$$

$$\text{Return on capital} = \text{Net profit before tax/total capital} * 100\% \qquad (1.5)$$

Tables 1.6 to 1.8 indicate that the share-type commercial banks have higher operational performance indicators than the state-owned commercial banks and policy banks. Clearly, the reason for this higher overall profitability is the fact that the share-type commercial banks are run along modern lines, with their ultimate objective being the maximization of profits. Their management is based on their asset–liability ratio, with clear property rights and flexible management mechanisms. At the same time, they have introduced the market mechanism into their management to a greater extent than the other types of banks. They are not subject to government interference, nor are they restricted by credit quotas, the requirement to make policy loans, and so on. Among the share-type banks, the most impressive performance has been displayed by China Merchants Bank, Shenzhen Development Bank, Shanghai Pudong Development Bank and China Everbright Bank.

Table 1.6 Performance Indicators for China's Banking Industry – Return on Assets (ROA), 1994–2001 (%)

		1994		1995		1996		1997	
State-owned Commercial Banks	Industrial and Commercial Bank of China	0.16	10	0.15	14				
	Agricultural Bank of China	0.09	11	0.35	12	0.32	13	0.05	17
	Bank of China			0.52	10	0.56	10	0.26	14
	China Construction Bank	0.20	9	0.36	11	0.31	14	0.11	16
Policy Banks	State Development Bank	–0.62	12	0.05	15	0.45	12	0.31	13
	Export–Import Bank			0.94	9	0.63	8	0.34	12
	Agriculture Development Bank			0.03	16	0.03	16	–0.26	18
Share-type Commercial Banks	Bank of Communication	**1.82**	**3**	**1.69**	**3**	1.45	7	1.16	10
	CITIC Industrial Bank	0.97	7	1.17	7	1.46	6	1.59	6
	China Everbright Bank	**1.60**	**5**	1.60	6	**1.89**	**4**	**2.66**	**1**
	Hua Xia Bank			**1.62**	**4**	**1.83**	**5**	1.32	8
	China Minsheng Bank					0.14	15	**2.11**	**3**
	Guangdong Development Bank	1.57	6	1.15	8	0.53	11	0.26	15
	Shenzhen Development Bank	**2.61**	**1**	**2.50**	**2**	**3.06**	**1**	**2.04**	**4**
	China Merchants Bank	**2.33**	**2**	**2.70**	**1**	**2.62**	**2**	**2.41**	**2**
	Fujian Development Bank							**1.98**	**5**
	Shanghai Pudong Development Bank	**1.81**	**4**	**1.61**	**5**	**1.92**	**3**	1.21	9
	China Investment Bank	0.25	8	0.23	13	0.62	9	0.51	11
	Bengbu Housing Savings Bank							1.36	7

Table 1.6 Continued

		1998		1999		2000		2001	
State-owned Commercial Banks	Industrial and Commercial Bank of China	0.11	17	0.48	9	0.44	6	0.34	10
	Agricultural Bank of China	–0.05	20	–0.02	19	0.01	16	0.05	18
	Bank of China	0.14	15	0.17	14	0.21	14	0.12	17
	China Construction Bank	0.11	16	0.33	11	0.34	9	0.19	12
Policy Banks	State Development Bank	0.19	14	0.15	15	0.25	11	0.41	8
	Export–Import Bank	0.28	12	0.24	13	0.23	13	0.12	16
	Agriculture Development Bank	0.05	18	0.14	16	0.30	10	0.14	14
Share-type Commercial Banks	Bank of Communication	0.55	9	0.50	8	0.42	7	0.38	9
	CITIC Industrial Bank	1.50	4	0.72	6	**0.62**	**5**	0.52	6
	China Everbright Bank	**1.74**	**2**	0.40	10	0.34	8	0.16	13
	Hua Xia Bank	0.99	7	**0.84**	**4**	**0.79**	**3**	**0.67**	**3**
	China Minsheng Bank	0.97	8	**0.99**	**1**			**0.65**	**4**
	Guangdong Development Bank	0.25	13	0.26	12	0.24	12	0.22	11
	Shenzhen Development Bank	**2.18**	**1**	0.60	7	**0.81**	**2**	0.47	7
	China Merchants Bank	**1.45**	**5**	**0.77**	**5**	**0.77**	**4**	**0.79**	**2**
	Fujian Development Bank	**1.55**	**3**	**0.89**	**2**	0.18	15	**0.58**	**5**
	Shanghai Pudong Development Bank	1.37	6	**0.85**	**3**	**0.94**	**1**	**0.83**	**1**
	China Investment Bank	0.43	10						
	Bengbu Housing Savings Bank	0.35	11	0.12	17				

Source: Compiled for this research.

Table 1.7 Performance Indicators for China's Banking Industry – Net Profit Ratio, 1994–2001 (%)

		1994		1995		1996		1997	
State-owned Commercial Banks	Industrial and Commercial Bank of China	0.73	11	0.72	14				
	Agricultural Bank of China	0.94	10	3.65	12	3.58	15	0.64	17
	Bank of China			8.43	10	8.94	9	4.16	13
	China Construction Bank	3.42	9	5.91	11	4.04	14	1.54	16
Policy Banks	State Development Bank	–15.24	12	0.63	15	4.55	12	3.67	14
	Export–Import Bank			13.33	9	8.27	10	4.18	12
	Agriculture Development Bank			0.13	16	0.15	16	–3.70	18
Share-type Commercial Banks	Bank of Communication	**26.04**	**3**	**22.15**	**4**	19.82	6	18.19	9
	CITIC Industrial Bank	15.95	7	16.20	7	17.72	7	**27.54**	**4**
	China Everbright Bank	**24.32**	**5**	17.15	6	**27.13**	**4**	**33.22**	**3**
	Hua Xia Bank			**29.61**	**2**	**34.24**	**3**	**25.25**	**5**
	China Minsheng Bank					4.15	13	**46.74**	**1**
	Guangdong Development Bank	17.73	6	13.54	8	7.01	11	3.61	15
	Shenzhen Development Bank	**25.62**	**4**	**24.09**	**3**	**35.25**	**2**	22.79	6
	China Merchants Bank	**33.29**	**1**	**35.74**	**1**	**35.84**	**1**	**34.46**	**2**
	Fujian Development Bank							15.56	10
	Shanghai Pudong Development Bank	**27.44**	**2**	**21.87**	**5**	**24.18**	**5**	18.58	8
	China Investment Bank	4.21	8	3.63	13	9.47	8	9.08	11
	Bengbu Housing Savings Bank							19.67	7

Table 1.7 Continued

		1998		1999		2000		2001	
State-owned Commercial Banks	Industrial and Commercial Bank of China	1.91	16	10.14	10	9.65	10	9.13	9
	Agricultural Bank of China	–0.78	20	–0.37	19	0.34	18	1.35	18
	Bank of China	2.50	15	3.66	14	2.22	17	2.95	16
	China Construction Bank	1.66	17	6.64	11	8.55	11	5.23	12
Policy Banks	State Development Bank	2.56	14	2.81	16	5.48	14	8.66	10
	Export–Import Bank	3.91	13	4.91	13	4.74	15	3.29	14
	Agriculture Development Bank	0.70	18	2.60	17	6.02	12	3.29	15
Share-type Commercial Banks	Bank of Communication	10.44	9	11.57	8	9.78	9	9.38	8
	CITIC Industrial Bank	**25.75**	**4**	**16.59**	**5**	**17.01**	**4**	15.24	6
	China Everbright Bank	**27.47**	**2**	11.18	9	4.70	16	4.49	13
	Hua Xia Bank	18.85	7	15.40	6	**22.57**	**1**	**20.22**	**1**
	China Minsheng Bank	21.88	6	**22.22**	**2**	13.60	8	**17.55**	**4**
	Guangdong Development Bank	4.57	12	5.57	12	5.85	13	6.15	11
	Shenzhen Development Bank	**30.56**	**1**	12.47	7	**18.04**	**2**	12.91	7
	China Merchants Bank	**27.23**	**3**	**18.92**	**3**	13.70	7	**20.11**	**2**
	Fujian Development Bank	17.85	8	**25.68**	**1**	**15.70**	**5**	**15.83**	**5**
	Shanghai Pudong Development Bank	**24.22**	**5**	**17.84**	**4**	**17.35**	**3**	**20.06**	**3**
	China Investment Bank	9.16	10						
	Bengbu Housing Savings Bank	6.79	11	3.45	15				

Source: Compiled for this research.

Table 1.8 Performance Indicators for China's Banking Industry – Return on Capital, 1994–2001 (%)

		1994		1995		1996		1997	
State-owned Commercial Banks	Industrial and Commercial Bank of China	4.84	9	5.04	13				
	Agricultural Bank of China	2.61	11	10.55	11	11.10	11	1.98	17
	Bank of China			14.74	10	14.63	8	6.70	12
	China Construction Bank	7.12	8	15.43	9	10.63	12	3.79	14
Policy Banks	State Development Bank	–1.25	12	0.23	16	3.01	14	2.57	16
	Export–Import Bank			6.96	12	5.40	13	3.10	15
	Agriculture Development Bank			1.45	15	1.52	15	–19.89	19
Share-type Commercial Banks	Bank of Communication	**29.83**	**1**	**27.89**	**4**	26.73	6	22.33	6
	CITIC Industrial Bank	16.78	7	21.72	6	**28.78**	**5**	**28.74**	**4**
	China Everbright Bank	**22.45**	**5**	**29.55**	**3**	**40.66**	**3**	**28.99**	**3**
	Hua Xia Bank			18.07	8	14.43	10	17.60	9
	China Minsheng Bank					0.86	16	**24.17**	**5**
	Guangdong Development Bank	20.86	6	18.80	7	15.64	7	6.17	13
	Shenzhen Development Bank	**26.54**	**2**	**25.93**	**5**	**36.29**	**4**	21.88	7
	China Merchants Bank	**26.42**	**3**	**38.64**	**2**	**40.92**	**2**	**39.56**	**1**
	Fujian Development Bank							16.97	10
	Shanghai Pudong Development Bank	**25.38**	**4**	**43.67**	**1**	**56.56**	**1**	**31.21**	**2**
	China Investment Bank	3.95	10	4.16	14	14.47	9	13.07	11
	Bengbu Housing Savings Bank							19.42	8

Table 1.8 Continued

		1998		1999		2000		2001	
State-owned Commercial Banks	Industrial and Commercial Bank of China	1.88	18	9.31	9	9.26	8	7.76	10
	Agricultural Bank of China	–0.68	20	–0.26	19	0.22	17	0.87	17
	Bank of China	2.52	15	2.96	15	1.72	16	1.42	16
	China Construction Bank	2.05	16	6.89	13	7.39	12	4.32	13
Policy Banks	State Development Bank	2.04	17	2.04	17	3.81	14	6.93	11
	Export–Import Bank	3.31	13	3.30	14	2.94	15	2.02	15
	Agriculture Development Bank	3.06	14	7.47	10	12.37	7	5.48	12
Share-type Commercial Banks	Bank of Communication	11.44	9	9.98	7	8.68	9	7.91	9
	CITIC Industrial Bank	**25.07**	**2**	**14.18**	**3**	**16.96**	**4**	**16.54**	**5**
	China Everbright Bank	**21.42**	**5**	7.33	12			3.31	14
	Hua Xia Bank	16.01	6	**16.10**	**2**	**22.24**	**2**	**23.70**	**2**
	China Minsheng Bank	14.80	8	**24.42**	**1**	7.19	13	**16.60**	**4**
	Guangdong Development Bank	6.01	12	7.44	11	7.90	11	8.07	8
	Shenzhen Development Bank	**23.31**	**4**	9.47	8	14.30	6	15.41	6
	China Merchants Bank	**24.30**	**3**	10.69	6	**32.49**	**1**	**41.25**	**1**
	Fujian Development Bank	15.58	7	**12.32**	**4**	8.61	10	12.36	7
	Shanghai Pudong Development Bank	**34.82**	**1**	**11.34**	**5**	**15.28**	**5**	**20.39**	**3**
	China Investment Bank	10.07	10			**19.13**	**3**		
	Bengbu Housing Savings Bank	6.50	11	2.46	16				

Source: Compiled for this research.

China Minsheng Bank has been affected by stock market listing; its performance was far superior in the three years prior to its November 2000 listing than the performance achieved since listing. The Bank of Communication has been performing poorly since 1996 and has been unable to make it into the top five. The fact that the ROA is markedly lower than the net profit ratio and return on capital shows that the main factor preventing China's banks from increasing their profitability is their excessively high non-performing loan ratio.

To summarize, although the state-owned commercial banks dominate the Chinese banking industry, they are affected by lack of clarity with respect to ownership, government interference, and so on. They also lack effective risk management and incentive mechanisms, and their internal controls are weak. As a result, their operational performance has been poor, and they have been unable to compete effectively against the share-type commercial banks, whose operations are based on the market mechanism. An excessively high non-performing loan ratio is a problem common to the whole of China's banking industry.

1.2 THE LIMITATIONS ON THE DEVELOPMENT OF CHINA'S BANKING INDUSTRY

Although there has been no large-scale bank failure in China, and no systemic payments crisis, individual banks have experienced crises, and there has been a systemic management crisis. This applies not only to the state-owned commercial banks, but also to the share-type commercial banks.

Restrictions Imposed on the State-owned Commercial Banks

On the surface, China's Ministry of Finance imposes the same financial management system on state-owned banks as on ordinary industrial and commercial enterprises; however, the wages and bonuses of employees in ordinary industrial and commercial enterprise are not subject to the same rigid controls as those in state-owned commercial banks. In ordinary enterprises, employee remuneration is linked to operational performance; in state-owned banks salaries are fixed, in the same way as those of government employees, and there is no relationship between salaries and the bank's operational performance. The only disparity is that salaries are higher in the economically developed coastal regions. Another difference is that, whereas ordinary industrial and commercial enterprises can decide for themselves whether to use their post-tax profits to expand their scale of production, in the state-owned banks decisions on reinvestment of profits are under the control of the Ministry of Finance. It is thus difficult for state-owned banks to gain full control over their own finances and over their own risk.

At present, China's commercial banking system remains an oligopoly, with inadequate competition and a system dominated by the state-owned commercial banks. Although the new share-type commercial banks have better opportunities for development and have been developing more rapidly, their market share is still very low. Another problem is that China's commercial banks are still largely restricted to deposit and loan business. The off-balance-sheet business, where banks provide financial services such as foreign exchange business, financial advisory service, agency business, cash card business, safety deposit box business and the like, in exchange for fees, is limited in scale, not properly regulated, and has little impact on banks' operating revenue. This is a clear departure from the operation of the commercial banks in the advanced nations, with their emphasis on cross-selling. China's banking business areas are not comprehensive or sufficiently broad (Zhou, Jiansong, 2000). For example, in 1998, interest income accounted for 98.8 percent of Industrial and Commercial Bank of China's total operating revenue, with handling fees accounting for only 0.67 percent of revenue (Jiao, 2002).

Furthermore, there is a lack of competition between the big four state-owned commercial banks, indeed they tend to act in collusion with one another. This is why the success or failure of the PBC's reserve policy, interest rate policy, loan policy, and so on, depends not on the PBC itself but rather on the extent to which the big four state-owned commercial banks are willing to collaborate with it. While all the state-owned commercial banks have improved the financial services that they offer to SMEs, having established dedicated SME lending divisions, many SMEs with great potential still find it impossible to secure bank loans. The main reason for this is that SMEs generally do not conform to the banks' asset–liability ratio and credit rating requirements, and the fact that the state-owned commercial banks' credit management mechanisms are not sufficiently flexible. Since loan investigations and authorization are handled by separate units, this tends to result in opportunities being missed and in the production of non-performing loans. Furthermore, punishments for errors in credit management are severe, while incentives are inadequate. As a result, state-owned banks tend to avoid those credit markets with a high level of risk. SMEs tend to require frequent and small loans, thus the cost of providing the loans is high, and the benefits are limited; state-owned banks thus tend to be unwilling to provide loans to SMEs (*Renmin Ribao*, 13 July 2002).

Savings are the main source of loan funding

During the process of institutional transformation, the role played by the market has remained limited. Most of China's banking system business is in domestic saving, estimated at close to 40 percent of GDP. State-owned banks are still mainly engaged in securing the retail deposits which are the main source of funding for their provision of low-interest loans. This excessive reliance on high-cost retail deposits will increase the banks' interest burden, thereby creating management risk (Huang, Min, 2000).

Excessively high non-performing loan ratio

The reasons why the non-performing loan (NPL) ratio of China's state-owned banks is so high include: (i) the reform of SOEs has been slow, and their operational performance is poor; (ii) the weakened state of the central government's finances means that the government is unable to provide the banks with sufficient financial assistance; (iii) local government authorities interfere in bank lending; (iv) the state-owned commercial banks are saddled with policy tasks; and (v) banks' internal risk control mechanisms are unsound (Liu and Luo, 2001). No one seems to know the exact scope of NPLs within China's banking system, since the PBC does not release sufficient data for confident assessment. But it is immense and swelling. Prior to 1998, Chinese banks had a unique loan classification system based on actual loan performance that split NPLs into three categories, namely, overdue, doubtful and bad. While this classification did not include highly risky bank loans that were still paying interest and were not yet overdue, it tended to underestimate NPLs. In 1999, China introduced an internationally accepted loan rating system, a five-classification loan structure – mention, pass, special mention, substandard, doubtful and loss – which is more stringent than the previous one. The new loan classification required all banks to categorize their loans according to the repayment ability of the borrowers and considered substandard, doubtful and loss as NPLs. While the PBC has set a very ambitious target for the big four state banks, they must reduce their ratio of bad loans by 2 percent or 3 percent a year to 15 percent by 2005, with NPLs fully provided for by reserves. As for city commercial banks and rural credit cooperatives, they must cut down their NPL ratios by 3 percent and 5 percent every year respectively.

Estimates of the size of China's state-owned banks' non-performing loans are shown in Table 1.9. If one accepts the highest estimate of 40 percent, then as of 1998, the big four state-owned commercial banks had total non-performing loans of RMB2,174.971 billion, accounting for approximately 27.3 percent of GDP. By the end of 2001, the big four state-owned commercial banks' non-performing loan balance had fallen by RMB90.7 billion since the beginning of 2001 (*Shichang Bao*, 24 January

2002). By the international standard classification, the ratio of the big four state-owned commercial banks' non-performing loan had fallen from 31.0 percent to 26.1 percent at the end of 2002, while most unofficial estimates were much higher, for example, 34 percent, 40 percent and 50 percent for Ernst & Young, Moody's and Standard & Poor's respectively (*Zhongguo Zhengjuanbao*, 21 February 2003). With regard to individual state banks, in 2002, the NPLs ratios fell from 28 percent to 22.4 percent, from 29.8 percent to 25.5 percent and from 19.4 percent to 15.4 percent for Bank of China, Industrial and Commercial Bank of China and China Construction Bank respectively (*China Daily*, 23 January 2003).

Table 1.9 Estimates of Chinese State-owned Banks' Non-performing Loan Ratios

Source of Estimate	Termination Date of Sample	Estimated Ratio (%)
Li Hsinhsin (1998)	1996	24.4
	Mid-1997	29.2
Chinese Economic Research Center, Beijing University (1998)	1997	24.0
Fan Gang (1999)	1998	28.0
Sung Chinghua (2001)	1998	40.0

Sources: Zhong (2001); Song (2001).

Low capital adequacy

In 1998, RMB270 billion worth of special government bonds were issued by the Chinese government, with the funds raised being used to increase the capitalization of the state-owned commercial banks. This, coupled with the efforts made in 1999 to deal with non-performing assets, resulted in a significant improvement in the big four state-owned commercial banks' capital adequacy ratios. In 1999 the average capital adequacy ratio for the big four state-owned banks was 6.19 percent, which was still less than the 8 percent required by the Basle Accord. However, the Bank of China had a capital adequacy ratio of 9.8 percent, and Industrial and Commercial Bank of China had a ratio of 8.98 percent, both of which exceeded the Basle Accord target (Liu, Jin, 2001). In 2000, Industrial and Commercial Bank of China were the seventh and eighteenth largest banks in the world respectively, with capital adequacy ratios of 8.12 percent and 8.31 percent. In 2000, the average capital adequacy ratio for the big four state-owned commercial banks was around 5 percent. In 2001, the PBC began to introduce strict controls with respect to capital adequacy, and as a result, all four of the big state-owned banks were required to achieve capital adequacy ratios of 8 percent in 2002, a target which meant that they would require an annual increase in capitalization of RMB50 billion (Wang, Zili, 2001).

Steadily falling profits levels

Looking at the banks' profit and loss statements, it is clear that while all the banks have been continuing to make a profit, profit indicators such as profit on capital (year-end assets/pre-tax profit) have been falling steadily. For the four big state-owned banks, profit on capital fell from 1.39 percent in 1985, to 0.4 percent in 1993 and to 0.1 percent in 1998. An even more serious problem is that while their profit and loss statements show that the state-owned commercial banks are still making a profit, in reality they are making a loss, their actual operational status is even worse than their profit and loss statements suggest.

Asset liquidity is inadequate

China's state-owned commercial banks have insufficiently high asset liquidity given that loan turnover has been falling. For example, in 1992, the Agricultural Bank of China had a loan recovery rate of 87.98 percent, but by 1998, this had fallen to 76.22 percent.

Limitations on the Operations of the Policy Banks

The problems faced by the policy banks include the following. Their scope of operation is limited to a handful of industries whose products are restricted to traditional loan business, and most of their loans are policy loans, particularly the provision of loans for the purchase and storage of agricultural products, basic industries, basic infrastructure and key construction projects, the importing and exporting of large items of equipment, and so on. Their loans have to conform to the requirements of national industrial policy, providing loan support for projects which the commercial banks are unwilling to support, i.e. projects which are not economically viable but are of benefit to society, with long repayment periods.

Furthermore, the policy banks are not permitted to set interest rates according to enterprises' ability to repay, which increases the level of operational risk they have to bear. Coupled with a disregard for profitability, lack of management experience and inadequate supervision, the quality of the policy banks' loan products has fallen. For example, in 1997, the Agriculture Development Bank made a loss of RMB2.5 billion; it was only with the provision of a government subsidy in 1998 that the Bank was able to get back into the black.

At the same time, there has been no decrease in the quantity of policy loans which the big four state-owned commercial banks are required to provide; this has affected the functioning of the policy banks. Apart from government subsidies, the State Development Bank and Export–Import Bank rely mainly on the issuing of bank debentures, while the Agriculture Development Bank relies on borrowing from the PBC to meet its funding needs. However, the interest rates and bank debentures term are all set by the PBC, which also orders other institutions to purchase them. The market mechanism thus plays little part in the policy banks' funding; the cost of raising capital is high, and the effectiveness of government's monetary policy is affected. As the policy banks lack sufficient branches of their own, they delegate much of their business to the commercial banks; however, the two parties' rights and obligations are not clearly specified in law (Li, Hongyan, 2001).

The Operational Risk Borne by the Share-type Commercial Banks

Owing to the difference in ownership structure, the state-owned commercial banks' risk is ultimately borne by the state, while the share-type commercial banks' risk is ultimately borne by the shareholders. Consequently, there is some variance in the willingness of these two types of bank to bear risk. If a share-type commercial bank is listed on the stock exchange, then the bearing of the risk extends further to include ordinary investors, but if bad management and poor risk management cause a bank to fail, this could be a serious danger to the health of the financial system as a whole (Zhang, 2000; Qu et al., 2001). The existence of the share-type commercial banks is beneficial to the promotion of regional economic development, helping to meet financing needs in different regions; however, the share-type commercial banks' branches and business tend to be concentrated in the coastal regions and the big cities, and their business scope is limited to traditional deposit, loan and settlement. Furthermore, the share-type commercial banks still suffer from serious weaknesses in the area of corporate governance. For example, the demarcation of responsibility between the Party Committee, the Board of Directors and the senior managers is unclear. At the Bank of Communication, the state's holding in the bank is so large as to give it complete control over the bank's operational management. At CITIC Industrial Bank, the bank's operations are under the control of the CITIC Group. The China Everbright Bank has the same phenomenon. Other problems include a lack of clarity in market positioning, and a failure to achieve differentiation from other banks. In addition, the mechanisms for operational management and risk control are not sufficiently sound, and the auditing departments lack the ability to undertake effective monitoring.

Latent operational risk includes a number of factors, and the operational status, asset quality and profitability of the surviving ten national commercial banks have been falling. The share-type commercial banks have a high non-performing loan ratio; at the same time, the tight monetary policy followed by the government since September 1997 has caused their share of the deposit market to fall. In addition, most companies have been experiencing substandard operational performance, pushing up the non-performing loan ratio of the share-type commercial banks. At the end of September 1998, the banks' non-performing loan ratio had exceeded the 15 percent limit set by the PBC; and by the end of 2000, the average non-performing loan ratio of the ten share-type commercial banks stood at 16.46 percent. However, by the end of 2001, it had been reduced to 12.94 percent (*Ta Kung Pao*, 6 February 2002).

At the same time, profit levels have been falling. In 1997, the banks' total pre-tax profit was RMB15.06 billion, falling to RMB11.54 billion in 1998, and RMB9.433 billion in 1999. In 1998, the average profit on capital was 1.13 percent, but by 1999, it had fallen to 0.647 percent. With the exception of Shenzhen Development Bank, Shanghai Pudong Development Bank and China Minsheng Bank, which were able to raise money on the stock market, the other share-type commercial banks had to rely on private subscription, retained earnings and conversion of shareholder bonuses and the like, to increase their capitalization. These methods of boosting capitalization are not suited to the banks' needs in terms of risk management in the expansion of their scale of operations. The majority of share-type commercial banks have capital of between RMB1 billion and 20 billion. Even the largest of them, Bank of Communication, has total assets equivalent to only 15 percent of the total assets of the Industrial and Commercial Bank of China. Thus the small size of the share-type commercial banks makes it difficult for them to achieve economies of scale. Furthermore, following the failure of Hainan Development Bank and several other financial institutions, the ability to secure outside funding among the ten share-type commercial banks operating nationwide has been reduced, as has the rate of increase in deposits. This has led to an increase in liquidity risk, exchange risk and profit risk.

As for the share-type city banks, at the end of 1999, there were 90 of them, with total assets of RMB553.8 billion. The city banks are local share-type commercial banks controlled by the local government authorities, with a level of operational risk that is even higher than that of the state-owned commercial banks and the share-type commercial banks operating nationwide. The main reasons for this high operational risk are as follows. At the end of 2000, the city banks' non-performing loan ratio was 31.06 percent, demonstrating the poor quality of their assets. Such accumulation of non-performing assets has reduced the city banks' liquidity and the proportion of their assets which are profitable, thus affecting their competitiveness. Some city banks have been making losses, which are steadily increasing, while some have very low capital adequacy ratios, reducing their ability to withstand risk. Others have too little capital to cover their debts, and are unable to repay them when they come due (Song, 2001; Deng, 2001).

China Merchants Bank[2] sought stock market listing in order to overcome the restrictions imposed by limited scale of operations. Stock market listing helped China Merchants Bank to get rid of non-performing assets, making it less burdened with 'excess baggage' than any other Chinese bank. Listing also allowed China Merchants Bank to increase its capital adequacy ratio, which in turn enabled it to establish more branches. Stock market listing also paved the way for the bank's strategy of internationalization. Following China Merchants Bank's listing, other small and medium-sized banks – including Hua Xia Bank, Bank of Communication, China Everbright Bank, CITIC Industrial Bank and Fujian Development Bank – also began planning to secure stock market listing. Nevertheless stock market listing is only a tool, not an end in itself. From the point of view of China's banks, the most important benefit of listing is that it forces them to respond to the requirements of the market and the external environment, encouraging them to focus on internal reorganization and on reforming their systems and mechanisms so that they can develop along healthier lines (*Guoji Jinrong Bao*, 25 December 2002).

The Operations and Operational Risk of Asset Management Companies

Although banks have replaced the government as the main source of financing for enterprises, the influence of the old planned economy is still being felt. Banks are required to meet SOEs' funding needs, and it is difficult for them to secure repayment of these loans. Furthermore, the effective interest rates on bank loans are very low, which encourages enterprises to invest more than they should, and with low efficiency. As a result, the corporate sector is loaded with debt which is increasing steadily; companies invariably end up having to take out further bank loans to cover their existing debt. The SOEs and state-owned banks are embroiled in a serious debt crisis; the high debt burden of the SOEs and the state-owned commercial banks' high levels of risk and low efficiency are threatening the normal operation of both the corporate and banking sectors (Xu, 2000).

If the banks' high non-performing loans ratios cannot be dealt with, this will have a serious impact on the operations of the Chinese financial system, affecting its future development. In order to solve this problem, in 1999, based on the Resolution Trust Corp. (RTC) model in the USA, China established four asset management companies (AMCs) – Cinda, Huarong, Great Wall and Orient – to handle the respective non-performing assets of China Construction Bank, Industrial and Commercial Bank of China, Agricultural Bank of China and Bank of China in an attempt to prevent a banking crisis. The four AMCs were set up as independent corporate persons wholly owned by the state, with total paid-in capital of RMB10 billion, all of which was provided by the Ministry of Finance. Their main task was to purchase, manage and dispose of the banks' non-performing assets, while seeking to maintain the value of the assets and keep loss to a minimum. These AMCs are intended to be a temporary measure, remaining in existence for only ten years.

The AMCs have been given various special benefits so as to enable them to dispose of non-performing assets efficiently. For example, they are exempted from payment of business registration fees, and from payment of all taxes relating to the purchase of companies and the acquisition and disposal of assets. They are also allowed to use a wide variety of different methods and financing channels to dispose of assets. These include asset conversion, transfer and sale, debt repackaging and corporate reorganization and securitization. They are allowed to issue bonds and commercial paper, to secure loans from financial institutions and to apply to the PBC for refinancing.

By June 2000, the four AMCs had acquired a total of RMB1.3 trillion worth of non-performing assets, accounting for between one quarter to three quarters of the big four state-owned commercial banks' total non-performing assets (RMB325.0 billion–433.3 billion per bank) (Lin, 2000). This total had risen to RMB1.3932 trillion by August 2000, with Huarong having acquired RMB407.7 billion of non-performing assets from the Industrial and Commercial Bank of China, Great Wall having acquired RMB345.8 billion of non-performing assets from the Agricultural Bank of China, Orient taking over RMB264.1 billion of non-performing assets from the Bank of China, and Cinda having acquired RMB375.6 billion of non-performing assets from the China Construction Bank (*Almanac of China's Finance and Banking*, 2001). As of 2002, the four asset management companies had disposed of a total of RMB301.4 billion of non-performing assets (excluding policy-type debt for equity swaps). The total value of recovered assets was RMB101.3 billion, giving an asset recovery rate of 33.61 percent. The total cash recovered was RMB67.5 billion, giving a cash recovery rate of 22.39 percent. Huarong disposed of a total of RMB63.15 billion, recovering RMB27.25 billion, to give an asset recovery rate of 43.15 percent; the amount of cash recovered was RMB19.79 billion, giving a cash recovery rate of 31.33

percent. Great Wall disposed of RMB106.03 billion, recovering RMB19.88 billion, to give an asset recovery rate of 18.75 percent; the amount of cash recovered was RMB9.82 billion, giving a cash recovery rate of 9.26 percent. Orient disposed of RMB45.46 billion, recovering RMB20.60 billion, to give an asset recovery rate of 45.32 percent; the amount of cash recovered was RMB11.24 billion, giving a cash recovery rate of 24.71 percent. Cinda disposed of RMB86.8 billion, recovering RMB33.59 billion, to give an asset recovery rate of 38.70 percent; the amount of cash recovered was RMB26.64 billion, giving a cash recovery rate of 30.69 percent (*Zhengjuan Shibao*, 23 January 2003).

Whereas in other countries the most common methods used for dealing with non-performing assets include sale, reorganization, securitization and conversion of debt to equity, China's AMCs have relied mainly on the conversion of debt to equity; the total amount converted is estimated to be around RMB40.5 billion. The conversion of debt to equity involves the AMC converting the commercial bank's non-performing assets into equity which it holds in the corporation in question. Sale or stock market listing is then used to realize this equity. This gets rid of the non-performing asset while also enabling the enterprise to increase its capitalization, reduce its asset–liability ratio and reduce financial expenses (Wu, Yue, 2000).

Taking 2001 as an example, Cinda's new disposals totaled RMB29.9 billion, with RMB10.488 billion in cash being recovered; a recovery rate of 35.1 percent. This was 17.5 percentage points up on the previous year, with expenses being kept strictly within the limits imposed by the Ministry of Finance. Total expenses came to RMB560 million in 2000, or RMB5.3 for every RMB100 of cash recovered. This was RMB3.97 lower than in 2000, a rate of decrease of 47 percent. Recovery of physical assets totaled RMB 600 million, RMB 5.1 billion down on the figure for 2000.

The total amount of assets disposed of by Great Wall was RMB53.106 billion, with cash value of RMB6.79 billion in 2001; the volume of assets recovered was RMB6.302 billion, accounting for 92.8 percent of present value. Of this, RMB3.69 billion was in cash, accounting for 54.3 percent of present value. Huarong disposed RMB12.8 billion of assets through international tender in 2001 (with Morgan Stanley), but settlement has yet to be completed. Huarong also disposed of a total of RMB23.21 billion in assets through debt restructuring, recourse, transfer, repackaging, auction, equity realization and offsetting of capital against debt, with the total amount of assets recovered being RMB12.54 billion, of which RMB7.55 billion was in cash and RMB4.99 billion in forms other than cash. The asset recovery rate and cash recovery rate were 54 percent and 32.5 percent respectively (*Jinrong Shibao*, 31 January 2002).

The biggest problem affecting AMC operation is the absence of a suitable market environment. State ownership of banks and enterprises means that the efforts of new investors are still hobbled by old systems. The underdevelopment of China's financial markets and lack of financial innovation both place restrictions on the methods that AMCs can use to dispose of assets. At the same time, the undeveloped state of intermediary institutions makes it difficult for AMCs to provide the necessary guidance services.

Most investments in China are very conservative in their attitudes, and the level of transparency with respect to information is very low. As a result, people lack the confidence to purchase non-performing loans. Furthermore, the prices for conversion of debt to equity are sometimes unreasonable; for example, some enterprises which are nominally making a profit, but in fact are making a loss, insist that their asset value be calculated at book value, rather than implementing transfer according to the actual net value.

There is also a lack of efficient exit mechanisms. Owing to the restrictions placed on the operations of AMCs, they need to divest themselves of their equity holdings as quickly as possible. However, at present this question is not being meaningfully addressed in China, and a sound equity exit mechanism has yet to be established; this raises the risk of moral hazard. If rigorous standards and time limits are not imposed on the conversion of debt to equity, then there is a risk of repudiation, whereby enterprises refuse to repay either their old or new debts, just sitting back and waiting for the conversion of debt to equity (Huang, Jinlao, 2000a; Wang, Xingyi, 2000). In addition, when disposing of assets through legal proceedings, AMCs often have to deal with interference by local government authorities, enterprise managers and the judicial authorities. As of the end of June 2001, of 1,052 cases brought, 544 had been settled, with the AMC being victorious in 543 cases. The total amount of debt repayment involved was RMB2.517 billion, but actual execution occurred in only 299 cases, with only RMB330 million being recovered (Jiang, 2002).

The most serious threat to China's banking system lies in the accumulation of NPLs. Without resolving the NPL problem, China's banking system will remain fragile and will face a financial crisis. The NPL problem will damage China's banking system beyond repair, thus the NPL problem must be solved. Resolving the NPL problem is crucial to sustaining economic growth. With China's entry into the WTO, there is also concern that the high level of NPLs of state banks may trigger a collapse of confidence in domestic banks, which could lead to a mass exodus of depositors to these foreign banks; the most imperative banking reform is, therefore, to find a thorough solution to tackle the NPL problem, both old and new.

China's WTO accession poses significant risks, as many SOEs are not in a position to compete effectively with foreign firms. State-owned banks in China will carry out government policy goals to finance the operations of SOEs, regardless of their profitability or risk; this moral-hazard lending will inevitably contribute to rising NPLs. Without a successful state-owned enterprises reform, new NPLs will emerge and further banking reform will be impeded, that in turn causes fiscal burden. In order to restrain flows of new NPLs in the banking system, there is a need to push SOEs reform forward – SOEs should be allowed to go bankrupt. And bankruptcy law should also be completely compelling to capably discipline unproductive SOEs. Within China's banking system, commercial banks are required to establish an information disclosing system to make their business information more transparent; hence, China's accounting rules should require that NPLs be fully disclosed and state banks should be granted the right to make the necessary loan loss provisions and loan loss reserves.

NOTES

1. The non-state sector accounts for 70 percent of GDP, but only 30 percent of bank loans. Clearly, access to funding is a major obstacle (Gong, 2002).
2. China Merchants Bank became the first bank in China to achieve stock market listing in accordance with standard international practice. The preparations for listing were conducted more rigorously than on any previous occasion.

2. The Evolution of China's Insurance Market

2.1 TRENDS IN THE DEVELOPMENT OF CHINA'S INSURANCE MARKET

With the establishment, in October 1949, of The People's Insurance Company of China, the Chinese insurance industry subsequently developed in line with the conversion, into state ownership, of all property. This process of nationalization was completed with the establishment, in 1956, of China Pacific Life Insurance Co., Ltd. During the period 1949–1958, the People's Insurance Company of China accepted a total of RMB1.6 billion in premiums, paid out RMB880 million in insurance proceeds, provided over RMB20 million for disaster relief, and paid RMB500 million into the national treasury, while the company itself accumulated a reserve of RMB400 million. In 1958, there were over 600 insurance offices throughout China, with a total of almost 50,000 people working within the insurance industry (Fan and Guan, 1999).

However, along with the implementation of nationalization, it was decided at the Third National Insurance Conference in 1953 and the Fourth National Insurance Conference in 1954 that the provision of compulsory casualty insurance would cease for government agencies, as well as for the railway, grain, posts and telecommunications, geology, irrigation and transportation sectors. Thereafter, at the Xian Financial and Trade Conference held in October 1958, it was announced that with the establishment of the People's Communes, there was no longer any need for insurance work; therefore, with the exception of overseas insurance operations, which would continue, all domestic insurance work would cease.

It was not until 1979, when the process of institutional transformation towards a market economy began, that the State Council gave its approval for the Conference of Branch Heads of the PBC to gradually revive domestic insurance operations. As a result, the People's Insurance Company of China began to restore domestic insurance operations in 1980, marking the rebirth of the Chinese insurance industry.

The People's Insurance Company of China comes directly under the State Council, and has registered capital of RMB2 billion. It main areas of business include: (i) the handling of various types of casualty insurance, life insurance, liability insurance, credit insurance and agricultural insurance business; (ii) the handling of various types of reinsurance; (iii) the handling of loss appraisal and claim business on behalf of foreign insurance companies, along with other related matters; (iv) the purchase, rental and exchange of movable property and real estate property related to the company's business.

The year of 1986 saw the establishment of the Xinjiang Production, Construction and Agricultural Production Insurance Company, to be responsible for arable and pastoral farming insurance for land farmed by the Xinjiang Production Corps; in 1992 this company was renamed the Xinjiang Production Corps Insurance Company. In 1987 the PBC gave its approval for the Bank of Communication and its branches to establish insurance divisions to undertake insurance business. In April 1991 the PBC ordered the separation of the banking industry from the insurance industry; as a result, the Bank of Communication's insurance division was spun off as China Pacific Life Insurance Co., Ltd. making it the second insurance company operating nationwide (after the People's Insurance Company of China). In May 1988 the Shenzhen Ping An Insurance Company was established in Shekou; in 1992 it was renamed the China Ping An Insurance Company, thus establishing the third insurance company to undertake nationwide operations in China.

In 1988 China began to experiment with specialized life insurance companies. Life insurance companies were established in various cities and provinces, including Zhuhai, Benxi, Xiangtan, Dandong, Guangdong, Shanxi, Tianjin, Fujian, Heilongjiang, Jiangsu and Yunnan. By 1995, seventeen specialized life insurance companies had been set up, and since the People's Insurance Company of China held shares in all of these life insurance companies, in following year, they were merged into the People's Insurance Company of China, which was reorganized as the People's Insurance Company of China Group, incorporating the People's Insurance Life Company of China, the People's Insurance Property Company of China and the People's Reinsurance Company of China (Li, 1998).

With these changes in the insurance system, the protection provided by state insurance was gradually lost, creating more demand for commercial insurance. During the two decades between 1980 and 2000, the Chinese insurance industry grew rapidly, at an average rate of 37 percent per annum, a rate far higher than China's GDP growth rate. From 1980 to 1990, there was over a 300-fold increase in premium income, and by 1999 there were four wholly state-owned insurance companies and nine share-type insurance companies, with a total of 8,745 branches and 172,892 employees. There were also fifteen foreign insurance companies, and two foreign intermediary companies. By 2001 there were four wholly state-owned insurance companies, sixteen share-type insurance companies, twenty foreign insurance companies and fourteen Sino-foreign joint venture insurance companies (see Table 2.1).

Table 2.1 Insurance Companies in China

Region	Name of Company	Form of Organization: Wholly state-owned	Share-type	Foreign-owned	Joint venture	Date of Establishment
Nationwide	People's Insurance Company of China	※				1949.10.20 1999.3.20
	China Pacific Casualty Insurance Company		※			2001
	Hua Tai Casualty Insurance Company		※			1996.8.29
	Pacific Casualty Insurance Company		※			2001.6
	China Life Insurance Company	※				1996.7.23 1999.3.19
	China Pacific Life Insurance Company		※			2001
	China Ping An Insurance Company		※			1988
	Xin Hua Life Insurance Company		※			1996.8.22
	Tai Kang Life Insurance Company		※			1996.8.22
	Pacific Life Insurance Company		※			2001.6

Table 2.1 Continued

Region	Name of Company	Form of Organization				Date of Establishment
		Wholly state-owned	Share-type	Foreign-owned	Joint venture	
	China Reinsurance Company	※				1999.3.18
Regional	Xinjiang Production Corps Insurance Company	※				1986
	Tian An Casualty Insurance Company		※			1994.10.22
	Da Zhong Casualty Insurance Company		※			1995.1
	Hua An Casualty Insurance Company		※			1996.10.18
	Yong An Casualty Insurance Company		※			1996
Foreign Insurance Companies	AIU (Shanghai) (USA)			※		1992
	AIU (Guangzhou) (USA)			※		1995
	AIU (Shenzhen) (USA)			※		1999
	AIU (Foshan) (USA)			※		1999
	Tokio Marine & Fire			※		1994.9
	Feng Tai (Shanghai) (Switzerland)			※		1996.12
	Qiu Bo (Shanghai) (USA)			※		2000.9.28
	Royal Sun (Shanghai) (UK)			※		1999

Table 2.1 Continued

Region	Name of Company	Form of Organization Wholly state-owned	Share-type	Foreign-owned	Joint venture	Date of Establishment
Foreign Insurance Companies	Mitsui Sumitomo (Shanghai) (Japan)			※		2001.6
	Samsung (Shanghai) (South Korea)			※		2001.4
	An Lian (Germany)					2001.9.25
	Ge Ning (Germany)					2001.9.25
	Zurich (Switzerland)					2001.9.25
	Royal Sun (UK)					2001.9.25
	Min An (Shenzhen) (Hong Kong)			※		1982
	Min An (Haikou) (Hong Kong)			※		1988
	Min Sheng Life		※			2000.10
	Dong Fang Life		※			2000.10
	Sheng Ming Life		※			2000.10
	Heng An Life		※			2000.10
	AIA (Shanghai) (USA)			※		1992
	AIA (Guangzhou) (USA)			※		1995
	AIA (Shenzhen) (USA)			※		1999
	AIA (Foshan) (USA)			※		1999
Foreign Insurance Companies (Joint Ventures)	Zhong Hong Life Insurance ∗Hong Li Life (Canada) holds a 51% share ∗A trust and investment company forming part of the Zhong Hua Group holds a 49% share				※	1996.11.26

Table 2.1 Continued

Region	Name of Company	Form of Organization: Wholly state-owned	Share-type	Foreign-owned	Joint venture	Date of Establishment
Foreign Insurance Companies (Joint Ventures)	Pacific Aetna Life Insurance ∗Aetna (USA) holds a 50% share ∗China Pacific Insurance holds a 50% share				※	1998
	An Lian Da Zhong Life Insurance ∗An Lian (Germany) holds a 51% share ∗Da Zhong Insurance holds a 49% share				※	1998
	Jin Sheng Life Insurance ∗An Sheng (France) holds a 51% share ∗China Lease (a subsidiary of China Wu Kuang) holds a 49% share				※	1999
	Kang Lian Insurance (Australia) ∗Kang Lian (Australia) holds a 50% share ∗China Life (Shanghai) holds a 50% share				※	2000.7
	Yong Ming Life (Canada) ∗Yong Ming Life (Canada) holds a 50% share ∗The Guang Da Group holds a 50% share				※	2000

Table 2.1 Continued

Region	Name of Company	Form of Organization				Date of Establishment
		Wholly state-owned	Share-type	Foreign-owned	Joint venture	
Foreign Insurance Companies (Joint Ventures)	Prudential (UK) ∗Prudential Life Insurance (UK) holds a 50% share ∗Zhong Xin Group holds a 50% share				※	2000.10
	Heng Kang Mutual (USA) ∗Heng Kang Mutual (USA) holds a 50% share ∗Tian An Insurance holds a 50% share				※	2001.2
	Zhong Li Insurance (Italy) ∗Zhong Li Insurance (Italy) holds a 50% share ∗China Petroleum and Natural Gas Group holds a 50% share				※	2000.7
	ING (Netherlands) ∗ING Group (Netherlands) ∗Zhong Liang Group				※	2000.7
	Quan Mei Life Insurance (USA)				※	2001.9.25

Table 2.1 Continued

Region	Name of Company	Form of Organization: Wholly state-owned	Share-type	Foreign-owned	Joint venture	Date of Establish-ment
Foreign Insurance Companies (Joint Ventures)	CPU International Assurance (UK)				※	2001.9.25
	National Life Insurance (France)				※	2001.9.25
	Jin Sheng Life Insurance (Sino-French joint venture)				※	2001.9.25
Total	54 companies	4 companies	16 companies	16 companies + 4*	14 companies	

Notes: 1. On 11 December 2001 US life insurance company AIG was granted four more licenses to establish branches in Beijing, Suzhou, Dongguan and Jiangmen.
2. If one adds in the four new AIG branches, the number of insurance companies actually operating in China is now 58.
3. The four additional companies are foreign casualty insurance companies, for which a separate category was not established.

Source: Insurance Industry Development Center (5 March 2002).

Insurance business in China can be divided into life insurance, casualty insurance, agricultural insurance and reinsurance. Life insurance can be subdivided into group insurance and individual life insurance; the categories of insurance provided include life insurance, accident insurance and health insurance. The main types of casualty insurance include business insurance, home insurance, vehicle and third-party insurance, aircraft and liability insurance, shipping insurance, cargo insurance, construction insurance and machinery insurance.

Reinsurance business can be subdivided into international reinsurance and domestic reinsurance. International reinsurance refers to business conducted between a domestic insurance company and a foreign insurance company in accordance with the relevant Chinese laws and international practice, and includes ceded reinsurance and assumed reinsurance. Domestic reinsurance refers to business conducted between the People's Insurance Company of

China and another domestic insurance company, including legal cession and voluntary cession. China currently operates a '2–8 system', whereby 20 percent of a domestic insurance company's risk is borne by a designated reinsurance company, with the remaining 80 percent being borne by the insurance company itself (Shi, 1999); however, because of the inadequate capacity of the Chinese reinsurance market, apart from the 20 percent compulsory reinsurance, most commercial reinsurance business cannot be handled within China. Another reason why there has been little growth in commercial ceding is the practice whereby Chinese insurance companies front for foreign reinsurers which are not authorized to operate in China. While on the face of it the risk is being taken on by the Chinese insurance company, in reality the whole risk is transferred to the foreign reinsurer. The Chinese insurance company can expect to receive around 5 percent of the profits. Because the rates for direct insurance in China are very high; most profits derive from premiums. There is thus little motivation for commercial ceding.

It is estimated that for various reasons, around 96 percent of reinsurance business is handled by foreign reinsurance companies. Taking 1998 as an example, in that year total cession fees in China came to US$72 million, of which only US$2.5 million went to Chinese reinsurance companies (Wang, 2002). A study undertaken by the China Insurance Regulatory Commission showed that, although foreign reinsurers are prohibited from undertaking RMB business directly in China, over 95 percent of ceding is in foreign currency and goes into the pockets of foreign insurance companies. China's dependence on the overseas reinsurance market is thus very high. At the same time, the lack of clear entry and exit mechanisms for the reinsurance market results in a tendency towards oligopoly. With no proper legal framework, it is impossible to implement effective supervision of the domestic reinsurance market (*Zhong Yin Wang*, 14 February 2003). Chinese reinsurers' total ceding revenue in 2002 came to RMB19.178 billion, 17.5 percent up on 2001. Ceding revenue from legally required ceding business came to RMB17.921 billion, 14.8 percent up on the previous year. Total commercial ceding revenue came to RMB1.266 billion, 76.08 percent up on 2001. Commercial property insurance ceding revenue totaled RMB957 million, while commercial life insurance ceding revenue totaled RMB309 million (*Zhong Yin Wang*, 13 February 2003).

During the period of transformation of the economic system towards a market economy, as financial deepening has progressed there has been a gradual easing of 'insurance suppression', a process which is generally referred to as 'insurance deepening'. The term 'insurance suppression' is used to refer to a situation where, following nationalization, enterprises and employees within the government system are protected, but those enterprises and employees outside the system have to rely on their own savings. The process of financial deepening can be measured using M2/GDP; while insurance deepening can be measured either in terms of insurance depth (annual premiums/GDP) or insurance density (annual premiums/total population). As can be seen from Table 2.2, financial deepening and insurance deepening have progressed in tandem (Deng, 2000).

In 1999, total premium income in China came to RMB139.322 billion, representing a growth rate of 11.7 percent. Total casualty insurance premium income came to RMB52.11 billion, an annual growth rate of 4.31 percent, and accounted for 37.4 percent of total premium income. Total life insurance premium income came to RMB87.21 billion, representing an annual growth rate of 27.74 percent, and accounting for 62.6 percent of total premium income. Total casualty insurance proceed payments came to RMB28.024 billion, representing a benefit payment rate of 53.78 percent, and an annual decrease of 3.56 percent. Total life insurance proceed payments came to RMB23 billion, representing an annual decrease of 3.5 percent.

By 2000, total premium income in China came to RMB159.59 billion, an annual growth rate of 14.5 percent. Total casualty insurance premium income came to RMB59.84 billion, an annual growth rate of 14.83 percent, and accounting for 37.5 percent of total premium income. The People's Insurance Company of China covered 77 percent of this business, Pacific Insurance 11.4 percent, and Ping An Insurance accounted for 7.9 percent. The three biggest insurance companies thus had a combined market share of 96.3 percent. Total life insurance premium income came to RMB99.75 billion, representing an annual growth rate of 14.38 percent, and accounting for 62.5 percent of total premium income. The People's Insurance Company of China accounted for 65 percent, Pang An Insurance accounted for 22.8 percent, and Pacific Insurance accounted for 8.4 percent. The three biggest insurance companies thus had a combined market share of 96.2 percent (Lu, 2001).

As of 2001, total premium income in China came to RMB210.94 billion, an annual growth rate of 32.2 percent. Total casualty insurance premium income came to RMB68.54 billion, an annual growth rate of 14.57 percent, and accounting for 32.5 percent of total premium income. Total life insurance premium income came to RMB142.4 billion, a growth rate of 42.76 percent, and accounting for 67.5 percent of total premium income. A total of RMB5.77 billion was paid in business income tax, giving realized profits of RMB5.06 billion.

Over the period January to November 2002, total premium income in China (domestic companies only) came to RMB273.77 billion, given an increase of RMB87.855 billion over the same period a year earlier, a rate of increase of 47 percent. Total life insurance premium income came to RMB202.88 billion, accounting for 74.11 percent of total premium income, at a growth rate of 65.15 percent on the same period in 2001. Total casualty insurance premium income came to RMB70.891 billion, accounting for 25.89 percent of total premium income, and representing a growth rate of 12.4 percent over the same period a year earlier (*Shichang Bao*, 17 December 2002).

Table 2.2 Financial Deepening and Insurance Deepening in China

Year	Financial Deepening (ratio)	Insurance Deepening (ratio)	Insurance Density (RMB)
1985	0.580	0.42	3.16
1986	0.659	0.65	4.95
1987	0.696	0.67	7.33
1988	0.677	0.72	9.30
1989	0.707	0.77	12.80
1990	0.825	0.85	15.52
1991	0.895	0.90	22.05
1992	0.954	1.00	31.40
1993	1.007	0.98	42.00
1994	1.004	1.13	41.53
1995	1.039	1.06	50.83
1996	1.121	1.10	61.93
1997	1.217	1.45	87.66
1998	1.314	1.56	99.94
1999	1.461	1.70	110.60
2000	1.506	1.80	127.70
2001	1.678	2.20	168.80
2002	1.807	3.00	237.60

Sources: Deng (2000); *Almanac of China's Finance and Banking* (2001); *Zhong Yin Wang* (22 January 2003); *Zhongguo Zixun Bao* (8 February 2003).

It is anticipated that over the next five years the average annual growth rate of the Chinese insurance market will be around 12 percent, so that by 2005, annual premium income will have reached RMB280 billion, equivalent to 2.3 percent of GDP. Of this, life insurance is set to account for around RMB190 billion, and group insurance for around RMB70 billion; there is thus considerable room for development in the insurance market (Wu, 2001; Sun, 2002). The number of insurance companies is growing, by five to ten companies a year, and by 2005 there may be close to one hundred in total (excluding agents and representatives) (*Zhong Yin Wang*, 3 July 2002).

Since the re-establishment of the Chinese insurance industry in 1979, as the economic system has been reformed and developed, as Table 2.3

indicates, insurance business has grown rapidly. In 1994, China was experiencing an economic downturn, this affected the development of the insurance market and since then the rate of growth in insurance business has slowed noticeably. Since 1995 the proportion of total insurance business accounted for by life insurance business has been rising steadily, while the proportion accounted for by casualty insurance has fallen; by 1997 life insurance accounted for a higher proportion of total insurance business than casualty insurance.

Table 2.3 The Development of the Insurance Business in China (Units: RMB Billion; %)

	Premium Income	Growth Rate (%)	Casualty Insurance Premium Income	Growth Rate (%)	Life Insurance Premium Income	Growth Rate (%)
1990	17.78	–	11.80	–	5.98	–
1991	22.74	27.87	14.42	22.20	8.31	38.96
1992	30.18	32.74	19.31	33.91	10.87	30.81
1993	39.55	31.05	25.14	30.19	14.41	32.57
1994	50.03	26.50	33.69	34.01	16.35	13.46
1995	59.49	18.91	39.07	15.97	20.42	24.89
1996	77.66	30.54	45.25	15.82	32.46	58.96
1997	108.80	40.10	48.60	7.40	60.20	85.46
1998	124.73	14.64	49.96	2.80	68.27	13.41
1999	139.32	11.70	52.11	4.31	87.21	27.74
2000	159.59	14.50	59.84	14.83	99.75	14.38
2001	210.94	32.20	68.54	14.57	142.40	42.76
2002*	273.77	47.00	70.89	12.40	202.88	65.15

Note: * The data are at the end of November 2002.

Sources: Li (1999); *China Insurance Yearbook* (2001); Sun (2002); *Shichang Bao* (17 December 2002).

The reasons for these changes are as follows: (i) the effective demand for insurance is too low. After more than ten years of rapid development, the pent-up demand for insurance, which had for so long been suppressed, has largely been satisfied. Furthermore, with the implementation of wholesale change in the housing and healthcare systems, the scope of social welfare has been reduced. Ordinary people now have to pay their own housing and medical costs, which has reduced the amount of money they have available to spend on insurance and other forms of consumption; (ii) businesses have been performing poorly. Many businesses have been faced with reorganization, and the need to lay off employees; their ability to pay insurance premiums has been reduced; (iii) owing to fierce competition in the industry, premiums have been reduced, leading to a significant reduction in premium income; (iv) insurance companies' expenses have remained high; (v) handling of claims is not properly regulated and the procedures are very complicated, leading to delay in payment; the current standard of claim handling service is barely satisfactory (Li, 1999). In 2000 the Chinese Consumers' Association complained that the insurance products available in Harbin, Nanjing, Zhengzhou, Wuhan, Xian and Lanzhou displayed a lack of innovation, and that insurance coverage scope and functions were inadequate; and (vi) insurance companies are poorly managed, thus costs are too high. One particular survey showed that 39.1 percent of consumers reported that excessively complex procedures were the main reason why they would not buy insurance products again (Yao, 2001).

Another point worth noting is that China covers a huge area, and regional disparities (in terms of economic development) are substantial. The coastal regions of Eastern China have reached a higher level of economic growth, and as a result, the development of the insurance industry has been more rapid within these regions. Economic development in Western China has been slower, and as such, the insurance industry there is less well developed.

There are also considerable disparities between the insurance market in urban and rural areas, owing to the limited access to information in rural areas, transportation problems, and differences in the general way of life. In rural areas, the population is more widely dispersed, thus the cost of providing service is higher, and educational levels are lower, making it more difficult for people to understand complex insurance products. This of course makes it more difficult effectively to develop insurance business in rural areas. In regional terms, insurance density and depth are highest in Beijing, Shanghai, Shenzhen, Xiamen and other coastal cities (see Tables 2.4 and 2.5). Taking as an example, Shanghai (where the insurance industry was opened up first), as of the end of 2002, there were 36 insurance companies operating. These included sixteen casualty insurance companies, eighteen life insurance companies, one insurance group, and one reinsurance company. There were fourteen insurance intermediary institutions, including three insurance brokerages, seven agencies, and four appraisal institutions. The total number of insurance institutions was thus fifty. Shanghai's status as an important financial center has led many insurance companies to locate their investment management centers there. Ping An and Hua Tai took the lead by establishing investment management centers in Shanghai; nineteen other insurance companies have since followed suit. Insurance premium income in Shanghai has also risen at an annual average rate of over 30 percent; for example, total premium income in 2002 came to RMB23.934 billion, RMB5.92 billion (or 32.86 percent) up on 2001. Total casualty insurance premium income came to RMB4.439 billion, RMB449 million (or 11.25 percent) up on 2001; total life insurance premium income came to RMB19.33 billion, RMB5.305 billion (or 37.83 percent) up on 2001. Total reinsurance premium income was RMB165 million, with 87 percent of this going to Chinese insurance companies and 13 percent to foreign companies (*Zhong Yin Wang*, 22 January 2003).

2.2 SUPERVISION OF CHINA'S INSURANCE INDUSTRY

Following the re-establishment of the Chinese insurance industry in 1980, with the gradual development of the insurance market, it became necessary to establish laws to regulate the industry. In 1985, the State Council promulgated the Provisional Regulations Governing Insurance Enterprise Management, specifying the types of insurance company that could be established, their organization, capitalization requirements, reserve levels, reinsurance requirements, and so on. These regulations gave responsibility for supervision of the insurance industry to the PBC. In 1991, the PBC published the Notification Regarding Insurance Oversight which was mainly concerned with the setting of insurance premium rates. The premium rates of insurance companies operating nationwide would require the approval of the head office of the PBC; but provincial branches would be allowed to raise or lower these rates by up to 30 percent. In the case of regional insurance companies, premium rates would have to be approved by the provincial-level branch of the PBC.

In 1992, in response to the establishment of AIG (Shanghai), the PBC formulated the Provisional Regulations Governing the Management of Foreign Insurance Companies in Shanghai. This stipulated the procedures for the establishment of new insurance companies in Shanghai, capitalization requirements and the scope of permitted business for foreign insurance companies authorized to operate there. In March 1995 the China People's Banking Law was enacted, establishing supervisory mechanisms for the financial sector and providing a legal basis for supervision of insurance companies. June 1995 saw the enactment of the Insurance Law which contained detailed provisions governing insurance companies, insurance contracts, insurance management, insurance industry oversight, and the operations of agents and representatives, providing for both judicial and administrative supervision of the insurance industry.

Table 2.4 Regional Insurance Density in China, 1998–2001 (Unit: RMB)

	1998						1999					
Region	Total		Casualty		Life		Total		Casualty		Life	
Shanghai	**788.00**	**3**	**248.80**	**3**	**539.20**	**3**	**885.97**	**1**	**263.82**	**3**	**622.15**	**1**
Shenzhen	**868.90**	**1**	**467.50**	**1**	**401.40**	**5**	**883.71**	**2**	**442.63**	**1**	**441.08**	**4**
Beijing	**808.52**	**2**	**226.66**	**4**	**581.86**	**2**	**730.61**	**4**	**226.93**	**4**	**503.69**	**2**
Xiamen	**782.00**	**4**	**322.00**	**2**	**460.00**	**4**	**803.35**	**3**	**342.66**	**2**	**460.69**	**3**
Ningbo	266.29	6	**130.49**	**5**	135.80	7	289.31	7	135.83	6	153.48	8
Tianjin	**282.40**	**5**	115.60	7	166.70	6	304.00	6	119.00	7	185.00	6
Qingdao	253.08	7	121.98	6	131.10	8	278.85	8	115.30	8	163.55	7
Zhejiang	172.73	9	71.88	9	100.85	9	165.00	10	80.36	9	115.91	9
Jiangsu	138.56	10	48.95	10	89.61	11	95.11	16	51.00	11	114.00	10
Liaoning							138.41	11	55.02	10	83.39	11
Fujian	106.49	12	47.99	12	**58.51**	**1**	57.00	30	49.96	12	67.05	13
Shandong	74.20	19	35.20	18	39.00	19	60.86	28	35.44	19	49.53	18
Heilongjiang	75.70	17	33.00	20	42.70	17	4.00	35	35.00	20	60.11	16
Jilin	90.50	13	40.20	14	50.30	14	104.00	14	40.44	15	63.60	15
Hubei	81.70	16	28.85	26	52.85	13	51.03	32	29.73	25	66.16	14
Yunnan	85.50	14	43.70	13	41.80	18	43.72	33	44.06	14	46.45	20
Inner Mong.	74.20	20	35.80	16	38.40	20	82.31	21	31.66	22	45.19	22
Ningxia	69.00	22	32.78	21	36.22	22	56.48	31				
Chongqing	74.41	18	30.30	22	44.10	16	82.65	20	32.68	21	49.97	17
Shanxi	69.00	21	35.00	19	34.00	23	77.00	22	36.00	17	41.00	25
Hebei	61.43	25	29.79	23	31.64	25	65.95	26	30.94	23	35.01	28
Qinghai	67.02	24	35.50	17	31.50	26	68.24	25	38.76	16	43.54	24
Shaanxi	67.03	23	29.05	25	37.98	21	90.51	17	28.45	26	46.00	21
Hainan	84.49	15	38.38	15	46.12	15	0.00	36	35.67	18	48.69	19
Gansu	59.22	26	29.33	24	29.89	31	74.45	24	30.77	24	37.47	26
Hunan	53.10	29	19.40	31	33.70	24	95.89	15	19.90	32	44.00	23
Sichuan	54.00	27	24.00	28	30.00	29	84.36	19	26.00	27	33.00	31
Guangxi	51.10	31	24.50	27	26.60	32	76.85	23	24.52	28	31.96	32
Jiangxi	53.11	28	22.31	29	30.80	27	117.01	13	24.17	29	36.69	27
Anhui	52.22	30	21.62	30	30.60	28	196.27	9	22.00	31	35.00	29
Henan	48.31	32	18.37	32	29.94	30	84.97	18	18.02	34	33.01	30
Guizhou	39.00	33	17.55	33	21.45	33	59.00	29	18.33	33	25.39	33
Tibet							22.67	34	22.67	30		
Dalian							**399.10**	**5**	**166.00**	**5**	**233.10**	**5**
Guangdong	181.40	8	83.40	8	98.00	10	63.90	27				
Xinjiang	116.17	11	48.28	11	67.89	12	119.24	12	48.29	13	70.95	12

Table 2.4 Continued

	2000						2001					
Region	Total		Casualty		Life		Total		Casualty		Life	
Shanghai	**968.80**	**1**	**270.00**	**4**	**698.53**	**1**	**1358.18**	**1**	**300.95**	**3**	**1057.27**	**1**
Shenzhen	**939.20**	**2**	**524.00**	**1**	**415.17**	**4**	**1156.67**	**3**	**578.99**	**1**	**567.62**	**4**
Beijing	**841.70**	**3**	**290.00**	**3**	**552.12**	**2**	**1277.00**	**2**	**276.00**	**4**	**744.00**	**2**
Xiamen	**780.50**	**4**	**338.00**	**2**	**422.39**	**3**	**998.06**	**4**	**377.55**	**2**	**620.51**	**3**
Ningbo	**339.10**	**5**	**146.00**	**5**	**193.25**	**5**	494.50	6	177.78	6	316.72	6
Tianjin	313.89	6	122.80	6	191.12	6	415.36	7	140.43	7	274.93	7
Qingdao	310.37	7	121.40	7	188.97	7	405.49	8	137.87	8	267.62	8
Zhejiang	241.46	8	96.93	8	144.53	8	343.86	9	115.50	9	228.36	9
Jiangsu	180.09	9	55.23	10	124.86	9	243.60	11	64.74	14	178.86	10
Liaoning	160.22	10	61.78	9	98.44	10	211.04	12	68.95	13	142.09	12
Fujian	131.79	11	53.03	11	78.76	11	198.74	13	71.03	12	127.71	13
Shandong	122.53	12	47.41	12	75.12	12	152.62	15	50.07	15	102.55	15
Heilongjiang	111.50	13	37.60	16	73.90	13	0.00	36	0.00	36	0.00	36
Jilin	109.27	14	40.32	14	65.95	15	132.39	16	43.52	18	89.07	16
Hubei	101.00	15	32.00	23	70.00	14	117.37	18	34.54	27	82.84	17
Yunnan	95.15	16	44.94	13	50.21	21	99.51	25	47.83	16	51.68	31
Inner Mong.	90.33	17	33.99	19	56.35	17	103.20	24	36.80	21	66.40	23
Ningxia	90.18	18	31.89	24	58.29	16	110.72	21	35.36	24	75.36	20
Chongqing	89.66	19	34.67	18	54.99	18	108.88	22	36.55	22	72.33	22
Shanxi	88.40	20	36.88	17	51.52	20	114.50	19	40.57	20	73.93	21
Hebei	83.89	21	32.19	21	51.70	19	114.01	20	36.36	23	77.65	19
Qinghai	83.19	22	39.92	15	43.27	25	104.43	23	44.22	17	60.21	24
Shaanxi	82.02	23	32.09	22	49.92	22	118.04	17	35.26	25	82.78	18
Hainan	77.05	24	31.28	25	45.77	24	93.58	26	41.23	19	54.36	26
Gansu	75.25	25	32.69	20	42.59	26	88.96	27	35.23	26	53.73	28
Hunan	71.03	26	21.49	31	49.54	23	84.71	29	24.84	33	59.87	25
Sichuan	70.00	27	31.00	26	39.00	30	86.78	28	33.00	28	53.78	27
Guangxi	66.57	28	26.27	28	40.30	28	73.69	32	27.97	31	45.72	33
Jiangxi	65.94	29	25.39	29	40.55	27	80.88	30	28.76	30	52.12	29
Anhui	60.76	30	23.32	30	37.44	31	76.64	31	25.61	32	51.03	32
Henan	58.78	31	18.96	33	39.82	29	72.80	33	20.74	35	52.07	30
Guizhou	45.40	32	19.60	32	25.80	32	53.30	34	21.96	34	31.34	34
Tibet	27.00	33	27.00	27			30.09	35	30.09	29	0.00	35
Dalian	2.10	34	0.80	34	1.30	33	**633.65**	**5**	**181.29**	**5**	**452.36**	**5**
Guangdong							249.06	10	95.76	10	153.30	11
Xinjiang							182.05	14	75.54	11	106.51	14

Source: Compiled for this research.

Table 2.5 Regional Insurance Deepening in China, 1998–2001 (%)

	1998						1999					
Region	Total		Casualty		Life		Total		Casualty		Life	
Beijing	**4.39**	**1**	**1.23**	**2**	**3.16**	**1**	**4.23**	**2**	**1.31**	**1**	**2.92**	**1**
Shanghai	**2.79**	**2**	0.88	6	**1.91**	**2**	**2.88**	**3**	0.86	6	**2.02**	**2**
Shenzhen	**2.66**	**3**	**1.43**	**1**	**1.23**	**4**	**2.49**	**4**	**1.25**	**2**	**1.24**	**5**
Yunnan	1.98	7	**1.01**	**3**	0.97	8	2.05	6	**0.99**	**4**	1.04	13
Xiamen	**2.37**	**4**	**0.98**	**4**	**1.39**	**3**	**2.42**	**5**	**1.03**	**3**	**1.39**	**3**
Tianjin	**2.01**	**5**	0.82	8	**1.19**	**5**	2.01	7	0.79	10	1.22	6
Qingdao	2.01	6	**0.97**	**5**	1.04	7	1.98	8	0.82	9	1.16	7
Ningxia	1.61	12	0.78	10	0.83	18	1.80	11	0.69	16	1.11	8
Gansu	1.70	10	0.84	7	0.86	14	1.86	9	0.84	7	1.02	16
Zhejiang	1.46	17	0.61	21	0.85	15	1.80	12	0.74	12	1.06	12
Shaanxi	1.56	14	0.68	16	0.88	13	1.76	14	0.67	19	1.09	9
Chongqing	1.58	13	0.64	20	0.94	9	1.71	16	0.68	18	1.03	15
Guizhou	1.70	9	0.77	11	0.93	10	1.78	13	0.75	11	1.03	14
Shanxi	1.34	22	0.68	18	0.66	26	1.50	20	0.70	15	0.80	24
Jilin	1.50	16	0.68	17	0.84	16	1.66	17	0.65	20	1.01	18
Qinghai	1.53	15	0.81	9	0.72	22	1.76	15	0.83	8	0.93	19
Ningbo	1.45	20	0.71	15	0.74	21	1.46	22	0.69	17	0.77	28
Jiangsu	1.38	21	0.49	26	0.89	11	1.54	19	0.48	29	1.07	11
Inner Mong.	1.46	18	0.71	14	0.75	20	1.43	23	0.59	21	0.84	22
Guangxi	1.10	27	0.53	22	0.57	31	1.17	31	0.51	27	0.66	32
Sichuan	1.20	25	0.50	24	0.70	24	1.29	27	0.57	23	0.72	29
Liaoning							1.40	24	0.56	24	0.84	23
Hubei	1.30	23	0.46	28	0.84	17	1.48	21	0.46	30	1.02	17
Jiangxi	1.20	24	0.50	23	0.70	23	1.31	26	0.52	26	0.79	25
Shandong	0.91	33	0.43	31	0.48	33	0.98	34	0.41	34	0.57	34
Hunan	1.07	29	0.39	32	0.68	25	1.23	29	0.38	35	0.85	21
Anhui	1.13	26	0.47	27	0.66	27	1.20	30	0.50	28	0.70	30
Heilongjiang	1.03	30	0.45	30	0.58	30	1.24	28	0.46	31	0.78	27
Hainan	1.45	19	0.66	19	0.79	19	1.36	25	0.58	22	0.78	26
Fujian	1.10	28	0.50	25	0.60	29	1.08	32	0.46	32	0.62	33
Hebei	0.95	32	0.46	29	0.49	32	0.96	35	0.45	33	0.51	35
Henan	1.03	31	0.39	33	0.64	28	1.05	33	0.37	36	0.68	31
Tibet							0.53	36	0.53	25		
Xinjiang	1.82	8	0.76	12	1.06	6	1.81	10	0.73	13	1.08	10
Guangdong	1.63	11	0.75	13	0.88	12	1.65	18	0.72	14	0.93	20
Dalian							**2.20**	**1**	**0.90**	**5**	**1.30**	**4**

Table 2.5 Continued

Region	2000						2001					
	Total		Casualty		Life		Total		Casualty		Life	
Beijing	**3.79**	**1**	**1.30**	**2**	**2.49**	**1**	**4.86**	**1**	**1.36**	**2**	**3.50**	**1**
Shanghai	**2.80**	**2**	0.78	7	**2.02**	**2**	**3.64**	**2**	0.81	8	**2.83**	**2**
Shenzhen	**2.44**	**3**	**1.36**	**1**	1.08	8	**2.77**	**4**	**1.39**	**1**	1.36	12
Yunnan	**2.06**	**4**	**0.97**	**3**	1.09	7	2.05	15	**0.99**	**3**	1.06	21
Xiamen	**2.04**	**5**	**0.89**	**4**	**1.16**	**5**	**2.41**	**5**	**0.91**	**5**	1.50	6
Tianjin	1.92	6	0.75	8	**1.17**	**4**	2.28	8	0.77	10	**1.51**	**5**
Qingdao	1.91	8	0.75	9	1.16	6	2.19	10	0.74	14	1.45	7
Ningxia	1.91	7	0.67	14	**1.24**	**3**	2.09	13	0.67	18	1.42	8
Gansu	1.89	9	**0.82**	**5**	1.07	10	2.14	11	0.85	7	1.29	17
Zhejiang	1.80	10	0.72	11	1.08	9	2.09	14	0.70	17	1.39	9
Shaanxi	1.76	11	0.69	13	1.07	11	2.34	6	0.70	16	**1.64**	**4**
Chongqing	1.74	12	0.67	15	1.07	12	1.93	18	0.65	20	1.28	18
Guizhou	1.71	13	0.74	10	0.97	17	1.86	20	0.77	11	1.09	20
Shanxi	1.70	14	0.72	12	0.98	15	2.11	12	0.75	13	1.36	13
Jilin	1.64	15	0.60	18	1.04	14	1.71	22	0.56	27	1.16	19
Qinghai	1.64	16	0.79	6	0.85	24	1.81	21	0.77	12	1.04	24
Ningbo	1.56	17	0.67	16	0.89	20	2.05	16	0.74	15	1.31	16
Jiangsu	1.54	18	0.47	26	1.07	13	1.88	19	0.50	29	1.38	11
Inner Mong.	1.53	19	0.58	21	0.96	18	1.60	25	0.57	26	1.03	26
Guangxi	1.52	20	0.60	19	0.92	19	1.57	26	0.60	22	0.97	31
Sichuan	1.51	21	0.67	17	0.84	25	1.70	23	0.64	21	1.05	23
Liaoning	1.45	22	0.56	22	0.89	21	2.01	17	0.66	19	1.35	15
Hubei	1.43	23	0.44	29	0.98	16	1.50	29	0.44	32	1.06	22
Jiangxi	1.41	24	0.54	23	0.87	23	1.55	27	0.55	28	1.00	28
Shandong	1.30	25	0.50	24	0.80	26	1.53	28	0.50	30	1.03	27
Hunan	1.26	27	0.38	32	0.88	22	1.40	31	0.41	34	0.99	29
Anhui	1.26	26	0.49	25	0.77	28	1.47	30	0.49	31	0.98	30
Heilongjiang	1.18	28	0.40	31	0.78	27	0.00	36	0.00	36	0.00	36
Hainan	1.17	29	0.47	27	0.70	30	1.34	33	0.58	24	0.76	34
Fujian	1.14	30	0.46	28	0.68	32	1.61	24	0.59	23	1.03	25
Hebei	1.12	31	0.43	30	0.69	31	1.37	32	0.44	33	0.93	32
Henan	1.09	32	0.35	33	0.74	29	1.23	34	0.35	35	0.88	33
Tibet	0.60	33	0.60	20			0.58	35	0.58	25	0.00	35
Xinjiang							2.30	7	**0.95**	**4**	1.35	14
Guangdong							2.25	9	0.87	6	1.38	10
Dalian							**2.84**	**3**	0.81	9	**2.03**	**3**

Source: Compiled for this research.

The Provisional Regulations Governing Insurance Agent Management, which came into effect in 1997, and the Provisional Regulations Governing Insurance Broker Management, which came into effect in February 1998, respectively sought to regulate the behavior of insurance agents and brokers.

Promulgation of the Regulations Governing Insurance Company Management, the Provisional Regulations Governing Insurance Actuary Management and the Temporary Regulations Governing Part-time Insurance Agent Management subsequently followed, in 2000, seeking to regulate the respective activities of insurance companies, insurance actuaries and part-time insurance agents. The method of supervision used for casualty insurance products was also adjusted with the formulation of the Temporary Regulations Governing Casualty Insurance Premium Rates, the first step towards product management reform. In March 2001 the Regulations Governing the Management of Insurance Company Minimum Repayment Capability and Oversight Indices were promulgated, marking the first attempt to regulate insurance companies' repayment ability.

Towards the end of 2002 the China Insurance Regulatory Commission promulgated a first set of fifty-eight administrative review procedures to be eliminated in accordance with the State Council Resolution on the Elimination of the First Set of Administrative Review Procedures. These included the qualification review for investment in securities investment funds by insurance companies, the insurance company working capital for overseas operation review, the review for the purchase of state-owned enterprise bonds by insurance companies, the review for the share of total insurance company investment which may be accounted for by investment in securities investment funds, the review of insurance company transactions with associates, the designation of reinsurance companies, the review of life insurance company life tables, the review of the qualifications of law firms, firms of accountants and firms of auditors to engage in insurance-related business, the review for upgrading of foreign insurance companies' representative offices to branch status, the review of insurance company fixed asset investment, etc. By abolishing these review procedures, the China Insurance Regulatory Commission was entrusting some of its functions to the market, partly in order to increase insurance company investment in securities investment funds and speed up the flow of insurance company funds into the capital markets. The Commission also introduced stricter requirements with respect to insurance company solvency (*Shichang Bao*, 11 December 2002). In 2003 the Commission published the Draft Regulations Governing Actuarial Methods for New Life Insurance Products; it was clear that the Committee intended to impose a rigorous actuarial system to ensure that insurance companies operated in accordance with the requirements of the law.

With regard to the regulatory organizations for China's insurance industry, the Provisional Regulations Governing Insurance Company Management promulgated in 1985, the China People's Banking Law enacted in 1995, and the Insurance Law, all stipulate that the PBC shall be the regulatory agency for the insurance industry. In 1994, the PBC set up an Insurance Bureau which was to be responsible for the regulation of insurance companies and the establishment of the necessary legal framework, and which includes an Auditing and Regulatory Department responsible for on-site auditing and examination of insurance companies. The main regulatory indicators included the minimum capitalization requirement, reserve requirements, premium rate management, fund utilization controls, minimum repayment capability management, and allocation to the insurance guarantee fund and public reserve fund. Provision is also made for intervention and sanctions. For example, if during an annual or other regular examination of insurance companies, any management irregularities or violations of regulations are discovered, the PBC has the right to rectify the matter, impose sanctions and, if necessary, take over the running of the insurance company. In 1997, it was discovered that Yong An Casualty Insurance had seriously inadequate capitalization and had committed serious violations of the law; as a result, the PBC took over the running of the company. This was the first time that the PBC had used its authority in this way to take over an insurance company.

In November 1998, the China Insurance Regulatory Commission was established, coming directly under the State Council, to be responsible for regulation of the insurance industry. The Commission is the regulatory authority for all commercial insurance business in China with its main tasks being as follows: (i) formulation of policies, laws and regulations relating to commercial industry, along with industry development plans; (ii) regulation of the management of insurance companies in accordance with the requirements of the law, and provision of guidance where necessary; (iii) investigation and handling of violations of the law and of regulations by insurance companies; (iv) maintenance of order in the insurance market; and (v) establishment of an insurance market evaluation and early warning system, as a means of preventing and reducing risk in the insurance industry (Shi, 1999; Shen, 2000).

As the insurance industry has developed, self-regulation has assumed increasing importance. The year of 1994 saw the establishment of the Shanghai Insurance Industry Association, quickly followed by the establishment of similar associations in Guangzhou, Shenzhen and Beijing. In September 1997, the members of China's insurance industry signed the National Insurance Industry Covenant; on 16 November 2000, under the supervision of the China Insurance Regulatory Commission, the China Insurance Industry Association was established with four working committees covering casualty insurance, life insurance, insurance intermediary and actuarial. With the establishment of the China Insurance Industry Association and the regional industry associations, the Chinese insurance industry now had the beginning of a unified regulatory system whereby the government handled regulation, individual companies implemented internal controls, the industry as a whole regulated itself, and society provided effective supervision (*Zhong Yin Wang*, 29 November 2001).

The regulation of the Chinese insurance industry has always involved a high level of government intervention. Examples include the following (Peng, 2000).

1. *High market entry barriers*: As far as initial capital is concerned, the Insurance Law stipulates that where an application is made to establish an insurance company to operate nationwide, the minimum registered capital shall be RMB500 million. For a company which will operate only within a specific region, the minimum requirement is RMB200 million. Furthermore, this must all be in the form of paid-in capital. This is far higher than the requirement for other types of company. According to Company Law, the minimum capitalization for a limited (share) company is RMB10 million, while for a limited liability company it is RMB500,000. It is also stipulated that the only permitted forms of organization for an insurance company are share-type limited company or wholly state-owned company. Foreign insurance companies wishing to operate in China must conform to the following requirements: (i) the company must have been in continuous existence for a period of at least thirty years; (ii) the company must have had a representative office in China for at least two years; (iii) during the year prior to the submission of the application, the company must have had total capitalization of at least US$5 billion.

2. *Strict regulations governing the business scope, insurance premium rates, policy clauses, fund utilization and repayment capabilities*: In terms of the scope of operation, insurers are not allowed to engage simultaneously in casualty insurance and life insurance business, and their activities may not extend outside regional limits. As regards the formulation of policy clauses, the Insurance Law stipulates that for the main types of commercial insurance the basic policy clauses and premium rates will be set by the regulator. Those policy clauses and premium rates which insurance companies are allowed to set by themselves must be submitted to the regulator for approval. There are also strict restrictions on insurance fund utilization; the Insurance Law allows insurance funds to be invested only in bank deposits, government bonds, bank debentures and mutual funds.

China's insurance industry has been developing from an industry run by administrative fiat under a command economy, towards an insurance market working in accordance with the principles of a market economy. During this process, various forms of national and regional insurance company have developed, including wholly state-owned companies, foreign-owned companies and share-type companies. As competition in the insurance market has become much more intense, in order to secure higher market share, insurance companies have been relaxing their requirements and their self-regulation; at the same time, the regulatory mechanism is far from perfect and various problems have developed as a result (Lu, 1998; Hu and Zhao, 1998; Da Peng Securities Project Team, 2000; Yao, 2000; Liu, Fei, 2001; Wang, Ping, 2001; Tan and Gao, 2001). These problems include delays in the establishment of insurance legislation; indeed, the establishment of the legal framework for insurance business is still in its early stages. Although an Insurance Law has been enacted, there is a lack of appropriate ancillary measures, such as an Insurance Industry Law, Law for the Management of Foreign Insurance Companies, a Reinsurance Management Law, and so on. This makes it difficult to protect the rights of insurance companies and policyholders. Some insurance companies have become government tools, using the power of local government authorities to force customers to take out policies, clearly a situation which distorts normal market competition. At the same time, competition is not properly regulated; indeed, as competition has become more intense, order has been lost, which can be seen in both price and non-price competition. In terms of the former, competition is based on premium rates, fees and commissions, and insurance companies make use of high fees, low premiums and high refunds. The latter involves the use of government power as a means of encouraging customers to take out policies.

Furthermore, insurance company funds are not used efficiently. Up until 1998, insurance company funds could be invested only in bank deposits or the purchase of government bonds; however, on 12 October 1998 the PBC gave its approval for insurance companies to participate in the national inter-banks loan market, and to buy and sell bonds. As of 1998, fund utilization by the big three insurance companies (the People's Insurance Company of China, Ping An Insurance and Pacific Insurance) was largely confined to cash and bank deposits; these accounted for 40 to 60 percent of total funds. In October 1999 the China Securities Regulatory Commission and China Insurance Regulatory Commission gave their approval for insurance companies to invest indirectly in the stock market through mutual funds (including both secondary market mutual fund purchase and sale and primary market investment in fund subscription). Nevertheless, the investment channels available to insurance companies are still too limited. With a fiercely competitive market in which insurance companies have to cut premiums in order to remain competitive, the restrictions on investment channels limit the insurance companies' profit sources. Added to this is the fact that interest rates in China are currently very low, hence those companies with extensive funds stuck in the bank are bound to be making a loss. At the same time, with policy business being the main source of revenue, the insurance companies' operational strategy has been affected. There is a shortage of expert fund management personnel, which is detrimental to the insurance companies' fund operations, because it makes it hard to expand the scope of investment or reduce risk.

In 2001, the average rate of return on insurance company funds in China was 4.3 percent, 0.7 percent up on the figure for 2000, and within the insurance industry there were sixteen insurance companies experiencing difficulties, with a total of RMB2.59 billion at risk (*He Xun Wang*, 5 February 2002).

Tax treatment varies between the different types of insurance company; for example, the income tax rate is 15 percent for foreign insurance companies, but 33 percent for domestic state-owned and share-type insurance companies. As far as business tax is concerned, in 1997 the rate for businesses in the financial sector, such as banks and insurance companies was raised from 5 percent (where it had stood since 1993) to 8 percent, increasing the tax burden for all insurance companies. Furthermore, there are no tax breaks for individual policyholders either. Since 2000, the rate of business tax which insurance companies are required to pay has been reduced by one percentage point for three years in a row. In 2003, the business tax rate for insurance companies stood at 5 percent (*Zhong Yin Wang*, 24 January 2003) (see Tables 2.6 and 2.7).

A sound insurance market has three elements, insurers, insurance intermediaries and those insured; however, the development of insurance intermediary agencies has been unsatisfactory. Insurance intermediaries include agents, brokers, appraisers and the like. The opening up of the insurance intermediary market could help to make the insurance market more efficient and increase market scale.

As a result of accumulated interest margin losses, low profit rates and inadequate injections of capital, Chinese insurance companies are suffering serious solvency problems. As of the end of 2001, the total accumulated interest margin loss of Chinese life insurance companies was over RMB50 billion. The average return on assets was 1.19 percent, far lower than the international average, which was 2.1 percent (Wang and Wei, 2002).

At present, however, apart from insurance agents, China's insurance intermediary market is limited to insurance consultants, most of which are small-scale enterprises engaged in agency business, having little impact on the intermediary market. As of the end of 2000, China had no properly regulated insurance appraisal agencies in operation. In late December 2000 the China Insurance Regulatory Commission held the first national examination for insurance appraisers, and in 2001 the Commission approved the establishment of the first insurance appraisal companies in Shenzhen, Beijing and Dalian (Huang, Qingming, 2002). In 2001 only 1 percent of premium income in China was obtained via insurance agencies; this compares to a figure of 60–70 percent in developed insurance markets overseas. Furthermore, the quality of insurance intermediaries varies dramatically. Up to June 2002, the China Insurance Regulatory Commission gave its approval for the establishment of 26 insurance appraisal institutions, 17 brokerages and 127 agencies, with the first insurance appraiser examination being held on 23 December 2000 (Chen and Yin, 2001; Wang, Anran, 2002).

Another problem is that premium rates are very high. Owing to the fact that rates are strictly controlled by the regulator, they have remained high and the insurance products available all tend to be very similar, with the majority falling into the category of comprehensive insurance. At the same time, the design of health insurance and endowment insurance products does not conform to consumers' real needs (Jiang et al., 2001).

To summarize, the restrictions on the use of insurance company funds means that premium income is the main source of revenue, and operating costs are high, factors which have ensured that premium rates remain high. As a direct result of the 20-year interruption in the development of the insurance industry, there is a severe shortage of talent in the areas of approval, claims, actuarial and investment business. Taking actuaries as an example, when the first actuarial exams were held in 1999 only forty or so people passed, leaving a shortage of 5,000 actuaries; clearly, therefore, it has not been possible to meet market demand.

As economic globalization and the internationalization of capital progress, the Chinese insurance industry will start to fall in line with international practice. China has a population of nearly 1.3 billion, of which just fewer than 500 million live in the cities, with the remaining 800 million or so living in the countryside. The population is aging, and families are getting smaller; thus, with the transformation of the economic system, demand for commercial insurance will increase steadily. However, at present, the Chinese insurance industry remains at a very low level of development. In 1998, the insurance density was US$11.4 and the insurance deepening was 1.5 percent. These are far lower than the figures for the USA (US$2,722.7 and 8.65 percent), Japan (US$3,584.3 and 11.73 percent), South Korea (US$1,033.6 and 13.87 percent) and Singapore (US$1,006.1 and 4.61 percent). That is to say, the Chinese insurance market clearly has considerable potential for growth (*Baoxian Zixun*, 2000).

Table 2.6 Taxation Policy with Respect to Insurance Companies in China

	Type of Tax	Casualty Insurance	Life Insurance	Notes
1980–1982				Initially, all insurance business was tax-exempt.
1983–1986	Income tax Adjustment tax Business tax	55% 20% 5% Calculation of adjustment tax is based on gross profits; in 1985 the rate was set at 15%. Income tax and adjustment tax went to the central government, while business tax went to the local government.	Long-term insurance business (including long-term health insurance) was exempt from all taxes.	Calculation of business tax was based on the combined total of premium income, interest on loans and handling charges.
1987–1993	As 1983–1986. However, income tax and adjustment tax revenue was shared by the central and local government authorities.			
1994–1996	Income tax	The income tax rate was set at 55% for the People's Insurance Company of China, 15% for foreign insurance companies (exemption in the first year, followed by 50% reduction in the second and third years; 5-year exemption for foreign insurance companies operating in special districts), 15% for insurance companies operating in special districts, and 33% for all others.	As 1983–1986	
	Business tax	5%, paid to local government.		
1997–present	The business tax rate was raised from 5% to 8% (5% going to the local government and 3% to the central government). Domestic insurance companies were required to pay a 5% surtax to the local government; foreign insurance companies were exempted from this. Other rates remained the same as in 1983–1986. In 2001 it was decided that the 3% business tax paid to the central government would be eliminated over a 3-year period; that is to say, the total business tax rate would be reduced to 7% in 2001, 6% in 2002 and 5% in 2003.			

Source: Li and Wei (2001).

Table 2.7 Taxation Policy with Respect to Policyholders in China

		Unit Policyholders	Individual Policyholders
1980–1996	Casualty	Vehicle insurance and corporate property insurance premiums can be listed as costs.	No income tax deduction permitted.
	Life	None.	
1997–present	Casualty	As 1980–1996.	
	Life	Additional endowment insurance purchased for employees can be listed as costs, up to a maximum of 5% of total wages.	

Source: Li and Wei (2001).

The life insurance market has particularly high potential, with endowment insurance and accident insurance set to become the most important types. As far as casualty insurance is concerned, as property rights are clarified and the legal framework is effectively established, demand for liability insurance will increase, and the proportion of total insurance business accounted for by guarantee-type insurance will rise; at the same time, as income levels rise, demand for vehicle insurance will increase. A State Council survey covering forty-six cities with a sample of 22,182 households showed that only 6 percent of households felt that they had a good knowledge of insurance. Insurance ranked fifth in expenditure items after savings, real estate purchase and the like; however, nearly 50 percent of households stated that they would consider purchasing insurance products during the next five years. Health insurance and endowment products were the most popular, with 76 percent and 50 percent of households respectively planning to buy these. This survey clearly demonstrated that the Chinese insurance market does indeed offer huge potential (*Shichang Bao*, 16 July 2002).

In the past, the influence of the planned economy has led to the view that protection on life, old age, illness, and death and disability were automatic rights. The responsibility for arranging endowment and health insurance, which in normal circumstances should be purchased by the individual or the household, was given to the work unit, which led to a rapid increase in group insurance sales. However, as the reform of state enterprises progresses, in the future, it is clear that most insurance will be purchased on an individual rather than group basis (Liu and Chen, 2000).

There are, however, several constraints on the development of the insurance market. In order to stimulate investment and consumption, the government has cut interest rates eight times since 1996, and at present, the interest rate on one-year deposits stands at just 1.98 percent. With interest rates remaining low, the return on savings-type insurance products has fallen, which has led to a corresponding decline in demand for these products. At the same time, demand for protection and health insurance products has increased. However, if we examine the structure of the Chinese insurance market, it is clear that the protection insurance market is very limited in size, and that the health insurance market is insufficiently developed, a situation which is affecting overall premium income. Low interest rates also mean that there is insufficient interaction between the insurance industry and the capital markets; thus insurance companies' interest losses will increase, and will in turn, affect their repayment ability.

Since many companies in China are performing poorly, this discourages them from taking out additional insurance, and leads to delay in the payment of premiums for existing policies. At the same time, it is unlikely that there will be any major breakthrough in vehicle insurance, household property insurance and other types of property insurance. The rate of increase in household income has fallen, and the reform of state enterprises has led to an increase in unemployment; which has resulted in a pronounced increase in the number of people cancelling policies, unable to extend policies, or seeing their policy become invalid (Yang, Fan, 2000).

Having premium rates set by the government violates the market mechanism and restricts the development of insurance companies. China covers a vast area, and the environment and level of economic development vary from place to place. If a unified national premium rate is applied everywhere for the same type of insurance product, then it will be impossible to reflect differences in the level of risk between regions. This is likely to result in a situation where premium rates are high, risk is low and protection is high, or where premium rates are low, risk is high and protection is low, leading to adverse selection (Zhu et al., 2001).

The reform of the Chinese insurance industry is being regulated by the Management Regulations for Insurance Company Fund Utilization, which was implemented by the China Insurance Regulatory Commission in 2002. As of the end of 2001, the total assets of the Chinese insurance industry came to RMB459.1 billion, but it was intended that this figure should be increased. The regulations also aim to promote the introduction of the share system in state-owned insurance companies and encouraging ownership by foreign and individual domestic investors, while also promoting the establishment of an independent board of directors system, and the establishment of a system for dialog between the China Insurance Regulatory Commission and the boards of insurance companies, so as to strengthen insurance company governance. The regulations are also designed to encourage the stock market listing of insurance companies, and to speed up the reform of the legal framework, for example, through the revision of the Insurance Law, the Law for the Punishment of Violations of the Law by Insurance Companies, and the

Regulations Governing the Management of Insurance Companies (*Zhengjuan Ribao*, 25 February 2002).

Analysis of Insurance Market Structure

Having analyzed the development of the system under which the Chinese insurance industry operates, along with the potential market risk and management efficiency, we shall go on to measure the level of market concentration in the Chinese insurance industry using the concentration ratio (CRn) and Herfindahl index, and data from *Zhong Jing Wang*, the *Almanac of China's Finance and Banking* for the years 1997–2001, and *China Insurance Yearbook* data for the years 1999–2002.

$$CRn = \sum_{i=1}^{n}(S_i) = \sum_{i=1}^{n} X_i \Big/ \sum_{i=1}^{m} X_i \qquad (2.1)$$

where n represents the number of insurance companies and m represents the total number of insurance companies.

$$H = \sum_{i=1}^{n} (X_i / T)^2 \qquad (2.2)$$

where n represents the number of insurance companies and T represents the total market size.

For comparative purposes, the insurance industry is divided into insurance companies operating nationwide, regional insurance companies, and foreign-owned insurance companies. The calculation results are shown in Tables 2.8 and 2.9.

China currently has fifty-eight qualified insurance companies, of which twenty-two are foreign-owned life insurance companies and sixteen are foreign-owned casualty insurance companies, compared with twenty domestic insurance companies. However, limitations on the scope of business and geographical area of operation have restricted the development of foreign-owned insurance companies in the China market. The CRn and Herfindahl index calculations show the high extent to which the Chinese insurance market is monopolized by a handful of companies; those companies operating nationwide have consistently accounted for a large proportion of total premium income, while the market concentration level of the foreign insurance companies has never exceeded 1.29 percent. Although the market concentration level of those companies operating nationwide has been falling steadily, which shows that their monopolization of the market is gradually weakening, the Chinese insurance market is still dominated by these companies.

Table 2.8 CR Index Values for the Chinese Insurance Market, 1997–2001 (%)

	1997	1998	1999	2000	2001
CRr for domestic insurance companies operating nationwide	99.29	98.31	98.05	97.65	97.84
CRr for domestic insurance companies operating regionally	0.68	0.68	0.70	0.84	0.77
CRr for foreign-owned insurance companies	0.03	0.87	1.03	1.23	8.31

Source: Compiled for this research.

Table 2.9 H Index Values for the Chinese Insurance Market, 1997–2001 (%)

	1997	1998	1999	2000	2001
Hr for domestic insurance companies operating nationwide	54.88	30.49	30.09	28.61	23.53
Hr for domestic insurance companies operating regionally	0.0012	0.0012	0.0012	0.0016	0.0013
Hr for foreign-owned insurance companies	0.00001	0.0035	0.0051	0.0068	0.0049

Source: Compiled for this research.

As far as barriers to market entry are concerned, policy obstacles are the main problem in the Chinese insurance industry. The Chinese government has subjected the insurance industry to rigorous controls in order to prevent competition and maintain the government monopoly on insurance business (Peng, 2000).

The Human Resources Structure of the Insurance Industry

In terms of age structure, regardless of whether one is considering domestic insurance companies operating nationwide, domestic insurance companies operating regionally, or foreign insurance companies, the bulk of employees are aged 35 or under. The proportion of employees aged 46 or over is noticeably higher among domestic insurance companies operating nationwide than among those operating regionally or foreign insurance companies, giving the former an older workforce; this may be related to the fact that appointments in domestic insurance companies operating nationwide are made by the government (see Table 2.10).

Table 2.10 Age Structure in the Chinese Insurance Industry, 1998–2001 (%)

		2001	
	Under 35	36–45	46–
Domestic insurance companies operating nationwide	50.59	33.34	16.07
Domestic insurance companies operating regionally	67.89	24.84	7.27
Foreign-owned insurance companies	88.60	9.07	2.33
		2000	
	Under 35	36–45	46–
Domestic insurance companies operating nationwide	53.62	32.45	13.93
Domestic insurance companies operating regionally	59.27	31.63	9.09
Foreign-owned insurance companies	89.64	8.86	1.49
		1999	
	Under 35	36–45	46–
Domestic insurance companies operating nationwide	53.47	36.30	9.44
Domestic insurance companies operating regionally	57.34	32.43	10.23
Foreign-owned insurance companies	86.43	10.72	2.85
		1998	
	Under 35	36–45	46–
Domestic insurance companies operating nationwide	51.07	35.48	13.46
Domestic insurance companies operating regionally	65.70	24.74	9.56

Source: Compiled for this research.

As regards the educational structure of the Chinese insurance industry, for both domestic insurance companies operating nationwide and domestic insurance companies operating regionally the bulk of employees are educated to junior college or senior technical school level or below; in foreign-owned insurance companies, the proportion of employees educated to university level is noticeably higher, whereas in domestic insurance companies (both nationwide and regional), the proportion of employees educated to junior high school level or below is noticeably higher than in foreign-owned insurance companies; this is clearly related to the fact that the superior governance mechanisms and higher salaries of foreign-owned insurance companies enable them to recruit higher-quality personnel (see Table 2.11).

Table 2.11 Educational Level Structures in the Chinese Insurance Industry, 1998–2001 (%)

			2001		
	PhD	Master's or other graduate study	BA or BSc	Junior college	Senior technical school or lower
Domestic insurance cos (nationwide)	0.07	1.32	19.23	43.64	35.74
Domestic insurance cos (regional)	0.21	2.51	19.49	46.41	31.39
Foreign-owned insurance cos	0.22	5.58	42.04	29.77	22.39
			2000		
	PhD	Master's or other graduate study	BA or BSc	Junior college	Senior technical school or lower
Domestic insurance cos (nationwide)	0.04	0.66	16.74	33.61	48.95
Domestic insurance cos (regional)	0.11	2.98	23.15	44.00	29.76
Foreign-owned insurance cos	0.22	5.19	43.25	29.08	22.26
			1999		
	PhD	Master's or other graduate study	BA or BSc	Junior college	Senior technical school or lower
Domestic insurance cos (nationwide)	0.01	0.36	10.54	24.07	65.02
Domestic insurance cos (regional)	0.16	2.82	19.77	43.99	33.27
Foreign-owned insurance cos	0.39	4.67	44.68	25.75	24.51

Table 2.11 Continued

	1998				
	PhD	Master's or other graduate study	BA or BSc	Junior college	Senior technical school or lower
Domestic insurance cos (nationwide)	0.0197	0.6412	10.4448	0.0000	56.4055
Domestic insurance cos (regional)	0.0797	2.3506	18.4064	0.0000	36.2151

Source: Compiled for this research.

As far as the hierarchical structure of Chinese insurance industry personnel is concerned, it can be seen from Table 2.12, that this is a classic pyramid structure. Owing to the restrictions imposed on their scope of business, foreign-owned insurance companies have a noticeably higher proportion of senior personnel than domestic insurance companies (both nationwide and regional). Human resources are an important source of competitive advantage in the insurance industry. It would appear that, in order to enhance the overall competitiveness of China's insurance industry, the quality of the industry's human resources needs to be improved.

Table 2.12 Personnel Structure of the Chinese Insurance Industry, 1998–2001 (%)

	2001		
	Senior personnel	Middle-ranking personnel	Junior personnel
Domestic insurance companies (nationwide)	3.33	39.69	56.99
Domestic insurance companies (regional)	3.59	40.76	55.66
Foreign-owned insurance companies	4.13	31.40	64.46

Table 2.12 Continued

	2000		
	Senior personnel	Middle-ranking personnel	Junior personnel
Domestic insurance companies (nationwide)	3.31	37.91	58.78
Domestic insurance companies (regional)	4.31	36.57	59.12
Foreign-owned insurance companies	5.19	31.11	63.70
	1999		
	Senior personnel	Middle-ranking personnel	Junior personnel
Domestic insurance companies (nationwide)	1.84	37.39	60.77
Domestic insurance companies (regional)	4.86	36.43	58.71
Foreign-owned insurance companies	5.66	39.62	54.72
	1998		
	Senior personnel	Middle-ranking personnel	Junior personnel
Domestic insurance companies (nationwide)	3.32	35.93	60.75
Domestic insurance companies (regional)	5.83	35.32	58.86

Source: Compiled for this research.

Analysis of Operational Performance in the Insurance Industry

For the purposes of this study, return on equity (ROE) and profit rate are used to analyze the operational performance of insurance companies in China.

$$\text{ROE} = \text{Net Profits/Shareholder Equity} * 100\% \quad (2.3)$$

$$\text{Profit Rate} = \text{Profits before Tax/Operating Revenue} * 100\% \quad (2.4)$$

As Tables 2.13 and 2.14 show, the profitability of the domestic insurance companies operating nationwide and the foreign-owned insurance companies is significantly higher than that of the domestic insurance companies operating regionally. The reason for this is that the foreign-owned insurance companies are run according to market principles, with clear ownership rights and flexible management mechanisms, while the domestic insurance companies operating nationwide have been able to monopolize the market to a large extent, benefiting from the restrictions placed on the scope of operation of the foreign-owned insurance companies.

To summarize, although in recent years falling interest rates have hurt the profitability of the domestic insurance companies operating nationwide (which are all state-owned enterprises), they retain their dominant position in the market, with the protection policy of the Chinese government restricting the scope of operation of the foreign-owned insurance companies. However, now that China is a member of the WTO, the restrictions on foreign-owned insurance companies' business areas and geographical areas of operation will be relaxed, and the market share held by the foreign-owned insurance companies will gradually rise, which is likely to have a negative impact on the operational performance of the state-owned insurance companies.

Table 2.13 Operational Performance Indicators for the Chinese Insurance Industry – ROE, 1997–2001 (%)

	1997	1998	1999
People's Insurance Company of China	**49.35**		**15.38**
China Life Insurance Company			**9.12**
China Reinsurance Company		**29.28**	
Pacific	4.85	5.77	6.31
Ping An	3.96	**18.66**	**11.26**
Hua Tai Casualty Insurance Company	**7.25**	8.15	7.72
Tai Kang Life Insurance Company	0.00	3.32	3.37
Xin Hua Life Insurance Company	**18.28**	2.74	0.45
Xinjiang Production Corps Insurance Company			2.99
Tian An Casualty Insurance Company	2.93	5.13	3.83
Da Zhong Casualty Insurance Company	**11.06**	4.62	4.08
Yong An Casualty Insurance Company	–7.73	–0.55	3.24
Hua An Casualty Insurance Company	4.76	2.65	2.10
AIG (Shanghai) (USA)		–44.33	–25.33
AIG (Guangzhou) (USA)		**106.35**	–123.98
AIG (Shenzhen) (USA)			
Mei Ya (Shanghai) (USA)		**17.65**	**18.21**
Mei Ya (Guangzhou) (USA)		0.83	–0.88
Mei Ya (Shenzhen) (USA)			
Tokio Marine & Fire (Japan)	**6.55**	5.83	0.43
Min An (Shenzhen) (Hong Kong)		**10.67**	**23.67**
Min An (Haikou) (Hong Kong)		–7.37	2.23
Zurich (Shanghai) (Switzerland)			–15.95
Pacific Aetna Life Insurance		–2.04	–17.37
An Lian Da Zhong Life Insurance			–5.09
Zhong Hong Life Insurance		–33.86	–25.35
Jin Sheng Life Insurance			–14.94
Royal Sun (Shanghai)			–6.14

Table 2.13 Continued

	2000	2001
People's Insurance Company of China	8.84	0.00
China Life Insurance Company	**13.02**	9.50
China Reinsurance Company	**47.01**	**27.03**
Pacific	8.55	**45.68**
Ping An	**27.66**	**27.30**
Hua Tai Casualty Insurance Company	6.31	7.10
Tai Kang Life Insurance Company	0.58	–3.93
Xin Hua Life Insurance Company	0.27	1.45
Xinjiang Production Corps Insurance Company	11.87	6.65
Tian An Casualty Insurance Company	3.01	3.46
Da Zhong Casualty Insurance Company	6.51	4.35
Yong An Casualty Insurance Company	4.14	4.32
Hua An Casualty Insurance Company	4.01	0.71
AIG (Shanghai) (USA)	–280.00	–69.23
AIG (Guangzhou) (USA)	150.93	**68.67**
AIG (Shenzhen) (USA)	–20.73	–46.43
Mei Ya (Shanghai) (USA)	**13.11**	9.01
Mei Ya (Guangzhou) (USA)	0.55	–0.62
Mei Ya (Shenzhen) (USA)	–0.94	0.16
Tokio Marine & Fire (Japan)	10.37	11.11
Min An (Shenzhen) (Hong Kong)	**23.81**	**28.86**
Min An (Haikou) (Hong Kong)	–14.34	0.81
Zurich (Shanghai) (Switzerland)	0.74	4.15
Pacific Aetna Life Insurance	–34.68	–72.22
An Lian Da Zhong Life Insurance	–10.59	–16.85
Zhong Hong Life Insurance	–23.25	–32.76
Jin Sheng Life Insurance	–30.83	–46.15
Royal Sun (Shanghai)	–6.00	–7.72

Source: Compiled for this research.

Table 2.14 Operational Performance Indicators for the Chinese Insurance Industry – Profit Rate, 1997–2001(%)

	1997	1998	1999
People's Insurance Company of China			3.99
China Life Insurance Company	1.55		0.32
China Reinsurance Company	0.00	4.63	
Ping An	0.78	1.96	2.41
Pacific	0.68	0.67	0.75
Hua Tai Casualty Insurance Company	**39.08**	**25.62**	**13.35**
Xin Hua Life Insurance Company	**7.09**	1.22	0.27
Tai Kang Life Insurance Company		0.02	1.90
Xinjiang Production Corps Insurance Company			2.23
Tian An Casualty Insurance Company	2.67	4.62	3.17
Hua An Casualty Insurance Company	**14.24**	**5.02**	3.17
Da Zhong Casualty Insurance Company	**11.96**	**7.34**	**6.41**
Yong An Casualty Insurance Company	–18.01	–3.97	**15.20**
AIG (Shenzhen) (USA)			
AIG (Shanghai) (USA)		–2.85	–0.83
AIG (Guangzhou) (USA)		–12.63	–3.73
Tokio Marine & Fire (Japan)	**14.28**	**8.03**	**9.82**
Min An (Shenzhen) (Hong Kong)		3.34	5.76
Mei Ya (Shanghai) (USA)		**11.84**	**14.93**
Mei Ya (Guangzhou) (USA)		2.17	–2.25
Zurich (Shanghai) (Switzerland)			–16.31
Mei Ya (Shenzhen) (USA)			
An Lian Da Zhong Life Insurance			–85.58
Zhong Hong Life Insurance		–68.25	–26.87
Royal Sun (Shanghai)			–73.70
Min An (Haikou) (Hong Kong)		–2.73	4.32
Pacific Aetna Life Insurance		–133.33	–100.00
Jin Sheng Life Insurance			–520.00

Table 2.14 Continued

	2000	2001
People's Insurance Company of China	2.05	0.00
China Life Insurance Company	0.50	0.32
China Reinsurance Company	6.81	4.33
Ping An	0.83	1.89
Pacific	5.87	3.78
Hua Tai Casualty Insurance Company	9.46	**9.30**
Xin Hua Life Insurance Company	0.11	0.80
Tai Kang Life Insurance Company	0.63	–1.88
Xinjiang Production Corps Insurance Company	8.55	4.12
Tian An Casualty Insurance Company	5.34	4.09
Hua An Casualty Insurance Company	4.71	0.48
Da Zhong Casualty Insurance Company	**9.58**	5.44
Yong An Casualty Insurance Company	**15.36**	**6.29**
AIG (Shenzhen) (USA)	–70.83	–39.39
AIG (Shanghai) (USA)	–1.88	–0.25
AIG (Guangzhou) (USA)	–4.11	–3.85
Tokio Marine & Fire (Japan)	**13.08**	**13.71**
Min An (Shenzhen) (Hong Kong)	**10.32**	**12.01**
Mei Ya (Shanghai) (USA)	**10.22**	**6.91**
Mei Ya (Guangzhou) (USA)	0.91	–0.82
Zurich (Shanghai) (Switzerland)	0.73	5.84
Mei Ya (Shenzhen) (USA)	–10.40	0.80
An Lian Da Zhong Life Insurance	–13.97	–33.31
Zhong Hong Life Insurance	–14.57	–8.39
Royal Sun (Shanghai)	–19.99	–12.99
Min An (Haikou) (Hong Kong)	–26.62	2.53
Pacific Aetna Life Insurance	–53.09	–18.51
Jin Sheng Life Insurance	–132.26	–52.34

Source: Compiled for this research.

3. The Impact of WTO Accession on China's Banking and Insurance Industries

3.1 THE BANKING INDUSTRY

The Opening Up of the Chinese Banking Industry

The term 'banking internationalization' refers to a situation where, in order to expand profits and avoid risk, banks expand their scope of operation from their home country, undertaking transnational operation in foreign countries. As economic globalization has progressed, the trend towards banking internationalization has become more obvious, and in response to changes in the overall environment and changes to systems, China's banking sector has gradually been opened up. During the period 1979–1982, foreign banks were permitted to establish representative offices in China, and from 1982 to 1989, various laws and regulations relating to representative offices and branches of foreign banks and Sino-foreign joint venture banks were implemented in the Shenzhen Special Economic Zone.

During the period 1990–1993, the geographical restrictions on foreign banks were relaxed. Thereafter, in March 1993, Shanghai's Pudong District was opened up to foreign banks, and beginning in August 1994, foreign banks were allowed to set up branches in Shanghai, Shenzhen and eleven other cities (Beijing, Shenyang, Shijiazhuang, Xian, Wuhan, Chengdu, Chongqing, Hefei, Suzhou, Hangzhou and Kunming). In early 1997 the People's Bank of China gave its approval for nine foreign banks operating in the Pudong district of Shanghai to engage in RMB business on a trial basis, in accordance with the Provisional Management Law for the Operation of RMB Business on a Trial Basis by Foreign Banks Operating in the Pudong District of Shanghai. In 1998 the People's Bank of China expanded the scope of the RMB business in which foreign banks were permitted to engage, giving approval for ten foreign banks to operate RMB business in the Pudong district of Shanghai and for another six to operate RMB business in Shenzhen, on a trial basis. In March 1999, the geographical restrictions on foreign banks were further relaxed and the number of cities in which foreign banks were allowed to operate was expanded from twenty-three (including Shanghai,

Tianjin, Beijing) to include all major cities. In August 1999, approval was given for the establishment of eight more foreign banks, and thus, twenty-five foreign banks were allowed to undertake RMB business.

On 11 December 2001, China finally became a member of the World Trade Organization (WTO), with its undertakings made in order to secure WTO accession beginning to come into effect beginning on 1 January 2002. WTO membership will encourage the further opening up of China's banking industry, thereby taking it to a new stage of development.

The bilateral agreements reached between China and the WTO member nations show that the main elements in the opening up of the Chinese banking industry will be as follows: (i) foreign banks will enjoy the same rights as domestic Chinese banks (i.e. national status) in certain specified regions; (ii) non-bank financial institutions will be allowed to conduct consumer loan and auto loan business; (iii) within two years after WTO accession, foreign banks will be allowed to provide RMB services to Chinese enterprises; (iv) within five years after WTO accession, foreign banks will enjoy full access to the Chinese market; (v) within five years after WTO accession, foreign banks will be allowed to conduct RMB retail business; and (vi) within five years after WTO accession, the restrictions on foreign banks in terms of geographic region of operation and type of customers will be abolished.

However, according to the bilateral agreements signed between China and the USA, American banks will enjoy additional benefits. Following China's accession to the WTO, American banks will immediately be allowed to provide all foreign exchange services to joint venture companies; within one year of accession, American banks will be allowed to provide foreign exchange services to Chinese customers, and Sino-American joint venture banks will immediately be allowed to provide financial services, including RMB business and retail business; within five years of accession, joint venture banks will be allowed to convert themselves into wholly foreign-owned banks.

The number of foreign banks operating in China has grown rapidly. In 1993, there were eighty-two banks with 208 offices. By 2000, there were 391 foreign banks operating in China, including 158 branches of foreign banks and 233 representative offices. The total assets of foreign banks in China came to US$34.434 billion, growing at an annual rate of 8.56 percent; their total liabilities came to US$31.795 billion, growing at an annual rate of 9.01 percent. In 2000, there were thirty-three foreign banks conducting RMB business, of which twenty-five were located in Shanghai and eight in Shenzhen. Total RMB assets came to RMB29.354 billion, growing at an annual rate of 161 percent; total loans came to RMB26.149 billion, growing at an annual rate of 289 percent; and total deposits came to RMB7.639 billion, growing at an annual rate of 40 percent (*Almanac of China's Finance and Banking*, 2001). Table 3.1 shows the regional distribution of foreign banks in China.

On 1 February 2002, the Foreign Financial Institutions Management Law came into effect. The Detailed Regulations Governing the Implementation of the Foreign Financial Institutions Management Law were promulgated shortly afterwards, and 2002 was the first year in which all restrictions on the operation of foreign currency business by foreign banks in China were lifted; as a result, the foreign banks enjoyed impressive growth. In March 2002 Citibank's Shanghai Branch became the first foreign bank in China to be authorized to conduct all types of foreign currency business. It also received approval to undertake a capital increment, increasing its capitalization to RMB590 million. Subsequently, another ten or so foreign banks secured licenses allowing them to engage in all types of foreign currency business; these banks included HSBC, Bank of East Asia, Hang Seng Bank and Nanyang Commercial Bank. The second stage of foreign currency account management reform was due to begin at seventeen foreign banks[1] in Shanghai on 20 November 2002, with the adoption of a foreign currency account information management system. Restrictions have been relaxed in several areas. For example, companies or agencies opening an account can apply to open several regular foreign currency accounts, both domestic and international remittances can be transferred into time deposits up to the maximum permitted account size, without the bank being required to report this, and annual inspection of the regular foreign currency accounts established by those banks already using the account information management system will no longer be required. Many foreign banks are planning to expand their operational network by establishing new branches in Shanghai, Beijing and other parts of the country. As of 10 January 2002, twenty-eight foreign banks operating in Shanghai had had their applications to increase their capitalization or working capital approved by the People's Bank of China; the total amount involved was US$506 million. As for Beijing, as of 8 November 2002, a total of nineteen foreign banks had established branches in Beijing, and another ninety-four had representative offices there. Beginning on 1 December 2002, foreign financial institutions in Guangzhou, Zhuhai, Qingdao, Nanjing and Wuhan were permitted to engage in RMB business, and foreign banks began applying to be allowed to operate RMB business in these cities. As of the end of September 2002, there were a total of 181 foreign banks operating in China, of which forty-five were licensed to engage in RMB business. The total RMB assets of foreign banks came to RMB47.797 billion; loans accounted for RMB38.5 billion of this (*Da Kung Pao*, 9 November 2002, 20 November 2002; *Guoji Jinrong Bao*, 15 November 2002, 21 November 2002, 12 December 2002).

Table 3.1 Distribution of Foreign Bank Branches in China (as of end 2001)

	Shanghai	Shenzhen	Beijing	Guangzhou	Tianjin	Dalian	Xiamen
Hong Kong	4	10	2	4	1	3	3
Japan	10	3	3	2	4	6	0
France	5	3	1	3	3	0	1
USA	4	1	4	2	1	0	1
Singapore	4	1	1	1	1	1	2
South Korea	3	0	1	0	4	0	0
Germany	5	1	1	1	0	0	0
Netherlands	3	2	1	0	0	0	1
UK	1	1	1	0	1	0	1
Thailand	1	1	0	0	0	0	1
Canada	0	0	1	2	0	0	0
Belgium	1	1	0	1	0	0	0
Australia	1	0	1	0	0	0	0
Italy	2	0	0	0	0	0	0
Austria	0	0	1	0	0	0	0
Portugal	0	0	0	0	0	0	0
Malaysia	1	0	0	0	0	0	0
Switzerland	1	0	0	0	0	0	0
Philippines	1	0	0	0	0	0	0
Total	47	24	18	16	15	10	10
	Qingdao	**Shantou**	**Zhuhai**	**Fuzhou**	**Wuhan**	**Chengdu**	**Haikou**
Hong Kong	2	2	1	2	1	0	1
Japan	1	0	0	0	0	0	0
France	0	0	0	0	1	0	0
USA	0	0	0	0	0	1	0
Singapore	0	0	0	0	0	0	0
South Korea	0	0	0	0	0	0	0
Germany	0	0	0	0	0	0	0
Netherlands	0	0	1	0	0	0	0
UK	0	1	0	0	0	0	0
Thailand	0	0	0	0	0	0	0
Canada	0	0	0	0	0	0	0
Belgium	0	0	0	0	0	0	0
Australia	0	0	0	0	0	0	0
Italy	0	0	0	0	0	0	0
Austria	0	0	0	0	0	0	0
Portugal	0	0	1	0	0	0	0
Malaysia	0	0	0	0	0	0	0
Switzerland	0	0	0	0	0	0	0
Philippines	0	0	0	0	0	0	0
Total	3	3	3	2	2	1	1

Table 3.1 Continued

	Kunming	Nanjing	Shekou	Suzhou	Xian	Yangpu	Chongqing	Total
Hong Kong	0	0	1	0	1	0	0	38
Japan	0	0	0	2	0	2	0	33
France	0	0	0	0	0	0	0	17
USA	0	0	0	0	0	0	0	14
Singapore	0	0	0	0	0	0	0	11
South Korea	0	0	0	0	0	0	0	8
Germany	0	0	0	0	0	0	0	8
Netherlands	0	1	0	0	0	0	0	9
UK	1	0	0	0	0	0	0	7
Thailand	0	0	0	0	0	0	0	3
Canada	0	0	0	0	0	0	1	4
Belgium	0	1	0	0	0	0	0	4
Australia	0	0	0	0	0	0	0	2
Italy	0	0	0	0	0	0	0	2
Austria	0	0	0	0	0	0	0	1
Portugal	0	0	0	0	0	0	0	1
Malaysia	0	0	0	0	0	0	0	1
Switzerland	0	0	0	0	0	0	0	1
Philippines	0	0	0	0	0	0	0	1
Total	1	2	1	2	1	2	1	165

Source: Zhang and Zhang (2002).

In addition, in 2001 the People's Bank of China announced that, beginning on 11 December 2001, foreign companies (non-financial institutions) would be permitted to establish wholly-owned or joint venture auto financing service companies to provide loans for vehicle purchase to consumers. Within five years, foreign banks will be permitted to offer automobile financing to Chinese residents. The relevant management regulations are still being formulated, but General Motors, Ford and Germany's Da Zhong Financial Services are all planning to move into the Chinese auto loan market, either through joint ventures or through wholly-owned subsidiaries (*Zhong Yin Wang*, 22 November 2002).

The Characteristics of Foreign Banks

The special characteristics of foreign financial institutions operating in China include the following. Foreign banks have been able quickly to start making a profit; indeed, most of them were already making a profit by the second year after establishment in China. The main reason for this is the high demand for financing in the non-state sector. Most of the foreign banks which have moved into China are leading Japanese, US, British or French banks with high capitalization. The restrictions imposed by the Chinese government limit their operations to coastal regions with high population density which have been opened up to foreign investment, and major cities which have reached a relatively high level of economic development (such as the Changjiang (Yangtze) delta, the Pearl River delta and the Beijing–Tianjin area).

At present, the majority of foreign banks operating in China have only one or two branches, or at most a dozen or so branches. In terms of scale of operations and network reach they lag far behind the leading Chinese banks, which have thousands of branches. Banks such as Bank of East Asia, HSBC and Standard Chartered, which have been very successful in on-line banking operations in Hong Kong, are now beginning to exploit on-line banking's advantages (low cost, and freedom from geographical restrictions) in China (*Da Kung Pao*, 12 November 2002).

The three types of customer to which the Chinese government allows foreign banks to provide services are corporate customers, institutional customers and individual customers. Most of the foreign banks' corporate customers are large state-owned enterprises (SOEs), local branches of leading transnational corporations, listed companies, and private companies and township and village enterprises (TVEs) which have reached a certain size and achieved superior operational performance. Institutional customers include mainly insurance companies, securities firms, investment funds, and the like. Individual customers are mainly white-collar workers with high income levels, and employees of government agencies and businesses with a steady income. The main business areas for foreign banks include international settlement business, foreign exchange investment, consulting services and foreign currency loans.

In the USA, Citibank's savings and loans business brings in around 20 percent of total profits. Nevertheless, off-balance-sheet businesses such as acceptance, credit checks, corporate creditworthiness appraisal, financial planning advice, foreign currency futures and options trading account for 80 percent of total profits. In China, commercial banks are heavily dependent on deposits and loans; off-balance-sheet businesses have been very slow to get off the ground. Off-balance-sheet businesses' shares of total profits at the four leading state banks are: Bank of China – 17 percent; China Construction Bank – 8 percent; Industrial and Commercial Bank of China – 5 percent; Agricultural Bank of China – under 4 percent. The average for the four leading state banks is approximately 8.5 percent (*Zhong Yin Wang*, 23 December 2002).

The Advantages and Disadvantages of Chinese and Foreign Banks

Chinese financial institutions suffer from under-performing assets, high operating costs and high non-performing loan ratios. In comparison with Chinese banks, foreign banks have a number of distinct advantages (Duan, 2000; Wu, Xiangjiang, 2000): (i) foreign banks have flexible management mechanisms; (ii) the larger foreign banks (such as Citibank, HSBC and Standard Chartered) already have well established global settlement systems and global customer service systems; (iii) with their advanced operational networks, high credit ratings and high innovation capability, they are able to introduce new financial products from overseas, using distinctive marketing methods to gain market share in the China market; (iv) foreign banks are customer-oriented, the customer is the focus of all bank activities, and the banks are constantly seeking to introduce new financial services and products to meet customer needs; (v) in the area of e-enablement, foreign banks are at an advantage in terms of technology, funding and manpower; (vi) foreign banks have large numbers of personnel with many years of experience in international financial markets; (vii) with their first-class training mechanisms and superior working environment and working conditions, they are able to headhunt talented employees from Chinese banks (including university graduates, graduate students and student returning from overseas); and (viii) foreign banks base their decisions as to where to open branches on analysis of economic regions and then are able to expand their scope of operations outwards from the cities where they are located. They, therefore, usually have first pick of the best customers, including large SOEs, transnational corporations, larger private companies, institutional investors and high-income consumers. The branch networks of the Chinese state-owned commercial banks are based on administrative regions, and their business scope is constrained by regional boundaries. However, the foreign banks have now started to relax the requirements for opening an account at one of their branches, so as to increase their customer base. Foreign banks which have adopted this strategy include Bank of East Asia,[2] HSBC and Citibank.[3]

Foreign banks also have strong deposit and loan development capabilities, and their loan quality is high. Since 1995, foreign banks' loans have been growing at an annual rate of over 20 percent. Higher loan quality means that the non-performing loan ratio is low; as of October 1999, 73.29 percent of foreign bank loans came under the 'normal' category, with 12.93 percent being on the watch list and 13.74 percent being non-performing loans (of which 6.84 percent were substandard, 6.17 percent were questionable and 0.73 percent had been recognized as lost). The non-performing loan ratio is far lower than that of Chinese financial institutions, which stands at 25 percent (Sheng, 2001).

Foreign banks have an advantage with respect to the development of wholesale business and off-balance-sheet business, which makes it easier for them to secure the business of foreign corporations. With their superior operational management and collaborative relationships with transnational corporations developed over a period of many years, foreign banks find it easier to secure off-balance-sheet business such as international settlement which offers high profits with low risk and low cost. At present, foreign banks have a market share of approximately 40 percent in the Chinese off-balance-sheet business market. Furthermore, most foreign banks are universal banks; they can conduct both commercial banking and investment banking business, which allows them to undertake offshore financial business, universal lending and full marketization of interest rates. Their diversified scope of business helps them to spread risk, and allows them to secure different types of customer.

A comparison of the business areas of foreign banks and Chinese banks is provided in Table 3.2, while Table 3.3 also demonstrates that the foreign banks still enjoy special privileges. With regard to the tax burden, business tax accounts for the bulk of the foreign banks' tax burden; however, in the special economic zones, foreign banks can benefit from a number of provisions, including business tax remission, a reduction in income tax rate to 15 percent, and exemption from urban construction tax and education surtax. They enjoy tax exemption during the first two years after establishment and tax rate reductions for three years thereafter. For Chinese banks, the tax burden consists mainly of business tax (at 8 percent), income tax (at 33 percent), and urban construction tax and education surtax (at 10 percent of the income tax payment).

At the same time, the domestic banks have a heavy social responsibility. They are required to handle fee collection in two main areas: (i) a total of fourteen areas specified by the State Council and related agencies including worker endowment insurance, personal housing fund, unemployment insurance, business license annual inspection fees, code number annual inspection fees, legal fees, asset appraisal fees, notarization fees, disabled persons' employment fund, enterprise registration fees, Internet address alteration fees, labor contract certification fees, tax registration fees and foreign exchange personnel examination fees; and (ii) fee collection for provincial governments and local governments at lower levels. The number of fee items handled varies from province to province, but the average is around thirty. Provinces with a particularly large number of fee collection items include Guangdong with sixty-nine, Henan with fifty-eight, Jiangsu with fifty-one, Hebei with forty-nine, and Sichuan with forty-three (People's Bank of China Tax Survey Team, 2000).

Table 3.2 *Comparison of the Scope of Business of Foreign Banks and Chinese Banks*

Chinese Banks	Foreign Banks
1. Collecting deposits from the public. 2. Granting short-term, medium-term and long-term loans. 3. Handling domestic and foreign settlement. 4. Handling discount of bills. 5. Issuing bank debentures. 6. Agency issue, agency acceptance, underwriting of government bonds. 7. Purchase and sale of government bonds. 8. Inter-banks loans. 9. Purchase and sale (and agency purchase and sale) of foreign exchange. 10. Provision of L/C services and guarantees. 11. Agency collection of fees and agency handling of insurance business. 12. Provision of safety deposit box service. 13. Other services approved by the People's Bank of China.	1. Foreign currency deposit. 2. Foreign currency loans. 3. Foreign currency discount of bills. 4. Approved foreign exchange investment. 5. Foreign currency remittance. 6. Foreign currency guarantees. 7. Import/export settlement. 8. Purchase and sale of foreign exchange (dealing and discretionary). 9. Agency conversion of foreign currency and foreign currency notes. 10. Agency handling of foreign currency credit card payments. 11. Safety deposit and safety deposit box business. 12. Credit checks and consulting services. 13. Other foreign currency business approved by the People's Bank of China
Comparison	
Business areas which the two types of bank have in common (limited to foreign exchange business in the case of foreign banks): 1. Deposit and loan business. 2. Discount of bills. 3. Settlement. 4. Provision of guarantees. 5. Purchase and sales (and agency purchase and sale) of foreign exchange. 6. Agency collection of payments. 7. Safety deposit and safety deposit box business. 8. Inter-banks loans (those foreign banks authorized to conduct RMB business are allowed to participate in the inter-banks loan market).	Differences: 1. Chinese banks can engage in bond business as specified in Articles 5, 6 and 7 of the Commercial Banking Law. 2. Chinese banks can undertake insurance business on an agency basis. 3. Foreign banks can undertake foreign exchange investment business (where approved). 4. Foreign banks can undertake foreign currency remittance business. 5. Foreign banks can undertake foreign currency bill conversion on an agency basis. 6. Foreign banks can undertake credit check and consulting business.

Source: Jiao (2000).

Table 3.3 Special Benefits Enjoyed by Foreign Banks Operating in the China Market

	Chinese Banks	Foreign Banks
Setting of foreign currency interest rates	*Chinese banks have to abide by the People's Bank of China regulations governing foreign currency interest rates. Only limited fluctuation is permitted, and the method by which interest rates are fixed is insufficiently flexible. *In loan business, Chinese banks are not allowed to collect management fees, commitment fees etc.	*Foreign banks do not have to abide by the People's Bank of China regulations governing foreign currency interest rates, giving them more flexibility in pricing; rates can be adjusted according to the level of risk, and greater increases and decreases are possible. *Foreign banks are allowed to collect management fees, commitment fees etc. for loan business.
Geographical restrictions	Individual branches can handle only those customers living within their specified district; cross-district operations are restricted.	While restrictions are placed on where a branch can be established, once it has been established there are no geographical restrictions on its operations. Foreign banks can make a particular city the base for inter-regional operations.
RMB inter-banks loan business	The maximum term for inter-banks loans is four months.	The maximum term for inter-banks loans is one year.
Accounting policy	Chinese banks are required to adhere to the financial institution accounting system formulated by the Ministry of Finance.	Foreign banks may adhere to their parent company's accounting policy (i.e. European or American accounting systems, or international accounting practice).
Risk fund appropriation	Appropriation must be made at 1% of year-end loan balance. Unused risk funds may not be withdrawn in the same year.	Appropriation may be made according to the level of risk, providing greater flexibility.

Table 3.3 Continued

	Chinese Banks	Foreign Banks
Suspension of interest policy	If a loan is overdue by one year or more, it will be classed as a non-performing loan and interest on the loan will not be listed in the accounts.	If a loan is overdue by 90–180 days, interest will no longer be listed in the accounts.
Tax treatment	Chinese banks pay business tax at a rate of 8% and income tax at a rate of 33%. They are also required to pay urban construction tax and education surtax (at 10% of the income tax payment).	Various levels of business tax exemption and remission are granted to foreign banks operating in special economic zones. The income tax rate for foreign banks is 15%, and they are exempt from payment of urban construction tax and education surtax.

Sources: Huang, Jinlao (2000b); Liu and Wu (2000).

Furthermore, there is a general shortage of off-balance-sheet business specialists among all the commercial banks and the Chinese government supervises its domestic banks much more rigorously than it does foreign banks. As most of the foreign banks are universal banks, their innovative products and services do not require approval by the PBC, whereas all new services offered by Chinese banks must gain such approval prior to their introduction.

From the above analysis, it is clear that WTO accession will have a major impact on both the competitiveness and security of the Chinese financial system. According to the estimates conducted by Liu and Wu (2000), the situation in terms of competition between Chinese and foreign banks in the first five years after WTO accession will be as shown in Table 3.4.

Table 3.4 *Market Share Forecasts for Chinese and Foreign Banks in the First Five Years after WTO Accession (%)*

		Current Situation		1–2 Years after WTO Accession		3–5 Years after WTO Accession	
		Chinese	Foreign	Chinese	Foreign	Chinese	Foreign
RMB Business	Deposits	100	–	80–90	10–20	80–90	10–20
	Loans	100	–	80–90	10–20	80–90	10–20
Foreign Currency Business	Deposits	84	16	80–90	10–20	70–80	20–30
	Loans	60	40	50–60	40–50	50–60	40–50
International Settlement		70	30	50–60	40–50	40–50	50–60
Credit Card Business		90	10	80–90	10–20	70–80	20–30
Financial Derivatives		–	–	10 or less	90 or higher	10–20	80–90

Source: Liu and Wu (2000).

The impact of WTO accession on the Chinese banking industry can be examined from a number of perspectives (Wang, Yuanlong, 2000; Ding and Tang, 2000; Yang, Tao, 2000; Yuan et al., 2000) as follows.

1. *Falling market share of Chinese banks*: As can be seen from the forecasts in Table 3.4, with China having joined the WTO, the foreign banks' respective market share in the foreign currency deposit and RMB deposit markets will rise to around 15 percent and 10 percent. The foreign banks' share of the foreign currency loan market will increase to over one-third, while their share of the RMB loan market will rise to around 15 percent. The foreign banks' market share in off-balance-sheet business may exceed 50 percent, and they will dominate the financial derivatives business and the investment banking market. Within ten years of WTO accession, foreign banks should have overall market share of one-third to one-half.

2. *Weakening profitability of Chinese banks*: Following China's accession to the WTO, foreign banks will be targeting transnational corporations, SOEs, government agencies, public utilities and other first-rate customers. With their high-quality service, advanced technology and steady stream of new products, the foreign banks will be very attractive both to ordinary consumers and to many Chinese enterprises. As a result, many first-class customers are

likely to switch from Chinese banks to foreign banks, which in turn may cause the Chinese banks' non-performing assets to increase. With the Chinese banks losing both market share and customers, their earning ability is sure to be reduced, affecting their profits. Competition from foreign banks will be particularly fierce in the personal financial services market.

At present, the service provided is roughly the same, most customers would choose a Chinese bank rather than a foreign bank, but if the service of the Chinese bank is unsatisfactory, then many people might switch to a foreign bank instead. Around 39 percent of respondents to a recent survey stated that if a foreign bank provided suitable service, they would be willing to try it. By and large, it is younger people, and those in higher income brackets, who are more interested in trying out a foreign bank (*Guoji Jinrong Bao*, 7 June 2002).

3. *Reduced liquidity of Chinese banks*: As the foreign banks move into China's financial markets following WTO accession, the low management efficiency of the Chinese banks will be further revealed. Given that, by international standards, equity as a proportion of assets is low and the fact that the ratio of loans to assets is high, the Chinese banks will find that their resources are not allocated efficiently enough, and that their operational performance is poor (see Table 3.5). This will clearly provide the foreign banks with an opportunity to take away significant business from the Chinese banks, gradually depleting the Chinese banks' funding sources. With the funds of the Chinese banks heavily eroded by non-performing assets, the foreign banks will be able to secure large quantities of deposits from both enterprises and consumers which will eventually have a serious impact on the liquidity of the Chinese banks.

4. *The problem of maintaining normal operations following WTO accession*: WTO accession will have a major impact on Chinese corporations. In the car, construction materials, communications, computer and traditional manufacturing industries, once the high tariffs and subsidies which these industries used to benefit from have been abolished, some firms will be too uncompetitive to be able to survive. This will make it impossible for the banks to secure repayment of many of their loans, making it hard for them to maintain normal operations.

Table 3.5 The Development of China's Banks – International Comparison (%)

Indicator	China	World
Profit on Assets	0.4	1.3
Net Interest Income/ Assets	2.6	3.9
Equity/Assets	4.3	10.6
Loans/Assets	76.5	54.5
Non-interest Expenditure/Assets	2.98	8.9

Notes: 1. All of the above figures are averages.
2. The world figures are based on data for 80 developed and developing nations covering the period 1990–1997.

Source: Zheng and Gao (2000).

5. *The policy banks will suffer most*: The majority of the policy banks' customers are concentrated in a handful of industries, while the commercial banks' customers are more widely dispersed. This means that the impact of WTO accession will be greater on policy banks than on commercial banks. The policy banks lack market-oriented management mechanisms. With their single area of business, limited branch network and bureaucratic management, they will find it difficult to compete in the future.

6. *Growing competition for small and medium-sized commercial banks*: Most small and medium-sized commercial banks are share-type banks with a limited branch network, concentrating mainly on traditional deposit, loan and settlement business. Besides, they have been affected by the restrictions on market entry imposed by the Chinese government, and by the artificial division of the market into distinct segments. When compared to the state-owned commercial banks, they are at a serious disadvantage in terms of scale of operations and branch network size. With increasing numbers of foreign banks moving into the China market and expanding into RMB business, the competition will become even more intense, and the small and medium-sized commercial banks' market share will gradually fall (Wang, 2000).

7. *The difficulty of strengthening supervision to reduce risk*: At present, in the regulation of foreign banks by the PBC, the main focus is on market entry, thus the systems needed for effective regulation of foreign bank operation are not yet in place. Once a foreign bank has established a branch in China, it can

develop deposit, loan and off-balance-sheet business anywhere in the country. That is to say, the geographical restrictions on foreign bank operation exist in name only. There are currently various problems relating to foreign banks. Their deposits tend to be significantly greater than their level of lending, with all surplus foreign currency being moved overseas for arbitrage; foreign banks often violate banking regulations by allocating less than they should to the deposit reserve. They are able to make use of their global networks to transfer profits out of the country to avoid tax, and they are frequently accused of engaging in unfair non-price competition. The quality of supervision of foreign banks is still low, and the legal framework is inadequate, and regulation of foreign banks is currently still based on the Management Regulations promulgated in 1994 and the Provisional Regulations for the Conducting of RMB Business by Foreign Banks in Pudong (Shanghai) promulgated in 1996. The necessary ancillary measures have not been established, and the regulatory standards applied to foreign banks vary from place to place.

There is also a lack of contact with the regulatory authorities in the foreign banks' home countries, making it impossible to achieve effective regulation. If, following WTO accession, the geographical restrictions on foreign banks are lifted completely, and then the increasing complexity of the banking structure and the increase in the number of innovative new financial products being introduced will lead to an increase in instability and systemic risk in the banking system. Where a foreign bank's head office or branches in other countries are badly run, this will have a knock-on effect in China, and there is also a risk that violation of banking regulations by foreign banks in China could lead to a financial crisis. It will thus become even harder for the PBC to exercise effective supervision.

8. *The difficulty of expanding overall control over the financial sector*: Now that China has joined the WTO, more foreign banks will move into China, and the scope of operations and volume of business of the foreign banks will be increased. This will affect the monetary policy and financial regulation policy of the PBC. As far as monetary policy is concerned, the PBC's monetary policy tools, mid-term and long-term objectives, and transmission mechanisms will all be affected, and the ability of the PBC to exercise overall control over the financial sector will be reduced. From a financial sector regulation standpoint, as more foreign banks move into China, increasing the number of players in the market, the task of managing risk will become ever more complex. The fact that foreign banks can obtain funding from the international financial markets to offset government monetary policy will have a major impact on Chinese monetary policy. Given the inadequate level of regulation, if fluctuations occur in the RMB exchange rate, those foreign

banks holding large quantities of assets in RMB denominations are likely to make the situation worse, affecting the stability of the RMB exchange rate. The entry of foreign banks into China's money market is likely to increase the risk of a financial crisis, making it more difficult for the PBC to exercise overall control.

However, from the point of view of China's domestic banks, WTO accession is not without its advantages since it will help to improve the management capabilities of Chinese banks in the following ways (Wang, Yuanlong, 2000; Huang, 2001). It will stimulate the introduction of competitive mechanisms; because foreign banks possess huge quantities of both funds and experience in the use of advanced management techniques, the entry of more foreign banks into the China market will encourage the introduction of the same kind of competitive mechanisms and rules as used in international markets. This will stimulate the development of the Chinese banking industry, helping to increase transparency with respect to lending, strengthen bank supervision, encourage the establishment of sound financial sector infrastructure, promote the modernization of financial systems and the establishment of the necessary legal framework, speed up the process of bank reform and improve the quality of service provided. It will also lead to a strengthening of international collaboration in bank supervision. Given the trend towards financial globalization, effective regulation of transnational banks depends on collaboration between the regulatory agencies in different countries. In order to achieve effective supervision of foreign banks and banks operating offshore, China's financial regulators will need to strengthen communication and contacts with the regulators in other countries.

The entry of more foreign banks will also encourage the flow of foreign capital into China. The establishment of more channels for the inflow of foreign capital should ease the shortage of capital which China will experience in the course of its economic development. At the same time, the WTO's principles of reciprocity and national treatment will reduce the barriers faced by Chinese banks in expanding their overseas operations. Chinese banks will be able to establish branches overseas directly, helping them to develop overseas business and stake their place in the international financial markets.

The unfavorable situation in which Chinese banks currently find themselves, in terms of their tax burden, does not conform to the principles of fair competition and national treatment. Following WTO accession, the tax burdens of Chinese banks and foreign banks will gradually be brought into line, making it easier for Chinese banks to compete. Furthermore, WTO accession also means that Chinese banks will become a part of the international financial market. They will therefore be required to abide by international management principles and practice, which should speed up the implementation of comprehensive risk control and sound internal control mechanisms.

On the basis of the above analysis, we can examine the internal strength and weakness and the external opportunity and threat (SWOT) of the impact of WTO accession on the Chinese banking industry.

The strengths enjoyed by the Chinese banking market are the current rapid transformation of the economy, the state-owned commercial banks' branch and settlement networks covering the whole country, the ability of Chinese enterprises to learn fast and to be able to respond rapidly to changing circumstances, and the fact that there is no shortage of overseas returning students with financial expertise and the ability to serve as senior managers. Share-type commercial banks benefit from clear ownership rights, and the fact that they operate according to market principles, seeking to maximize profits, makes them more competitive. Furthermore, over a period of many years a close collaborative relationship has been established between Chinese banks, Chinese enterprises and the general public. Customers tend to feel alienated from foreign banks, giving domestic Chinese banks a cultural advantage.

The weaknesses of the Chinese banking industry include the relatively low level of education of Chinese bank employees resulting in a lack of knowledge about international financial practice and management techniques. The banks' training mechanisms are also inadequate. Another problem for the Chinese banking industry is that because foreign banks are unfamiliar with circumstances in China, they need to recruit managers and marketing personnel who are familiar with the local market. They can offer high salaries, the opportunity to undergo training overseas, a comfortable working environment and other advantages, and are thus able to headhunt large numbers of talented Chinese bank employees. For the state-owned Chinese banks, which lacked high-quality human resources to start with, this is making a bad situation even worse.

Other problems affecting the state-owned banks include the lack of clarity in ownership rights, the high non-performing loan ratio, inadequate development of new financial products, unsatisfactory internal risk controls and poor appraisal of loan customers. The poor operational performance of the state-owned commercial banks is an obstacle to raising the competitiveness of the banking industry as a whole. The high level of concentration in the market and the government policy of protecting state-owned banks are an obstacle to market entry by foreign banks, and they also make it harder for Chinese banks to increase their competitiveness. For example, in the opening up of the financial services market the Chinese government has quite clearly favored local companies.

Although the BOC International is nominally a Sino-foreign joint venture, the fact that it is in reality a domestic enterprise has enabled it to secure special treatment throughout China. BOC International has a 49 percent share in BOC International Holdings Limited. According to China's WTO pre-accession agreements, the share that foreign companies may hold in Chinese securities firms is to be increased in three stages, from 33 percent immediately after accession, to 49 percent within three years, and 51 percent within five years; viewed in light of this timetable, the share which BOC International holds in BOC International Holdings Limited seems very high. In comparison with BOC International Holdings Limited, it is clear that China International Finance Company has not received such favorable treatment. China International Finance Company was the first joint venture investment bank to be established in China, with Morgan Stanley and China Construction Bank each holding a 35 percent share, and the total foreign shareholding amounting to 50 percent. The attitude taken to this by the Shanghai Securities Administration Office was that 'this represents early implementation of the undertakings made by China in its pre-accession agreements; it is not a violation of the existing review standards for the establishment of joint venture securities firms' (*Guoji Jinrong Bao*, 1 April 2002).

In the future, as transnational corporations move into the China market, there will be high demand for financing. The presence of more foreign banks and the introduction of competitive mechanisms will help to improve the competitiveness of China's banking industry, helping it to fall in line with international standards. Furthermore, after China has joined the WTO, the tax burden will be made uniform between Chinese banks and foreign banks, so that the two categories of bank can compete on a level playing field. This should speed up the accumulation of capital by Chinese banks, thereby helping to enhance their competitiveness. WTO accession means that banks in China will be required to conform to normal international practice; China will have to implement banking sector regulation in accordance with the Basle Agreement. This should lead to an across-the-board improvement in risk management, the establishment of comprehensive internal control systems and the improvement of disclosure systems; financial sector supervision will become more comprehensive and more regularized, ensuring that it operates continuously and effectively. This will lead to an enhancement of the quality of management in the banking sector, while also facilitating the establishment of a fair and objective financial supervision system and the improvement of the business environment in the banking sector.

WTO accession will also help Chinese banks to develop their overseas business, and create new channels for drawing foreign capital into China.

However, the opening up of the banking market which WTO accession will bring, will result in a gradual increase in the market share of foreign banks. The increasingly fierce competition from foreign banks will increase the level of risk which Chinese banks have to bear, and make it more difficult for the PBC to exercise its regulatory function (see Table 3.6).

Table 3.6 SWOT Analysis of the Chinese Banking Industry

Strengths	Weaknesses
* An extensive branch network. * Enterprises are quick to learn and adjust. * Share-type commercial banks are highly competitive. * Cultural identity – customers prefer to work with a Chinese bank.	* Lack of international finance talent, and lack of necessary management techniques. * High non-performing loan ratio. * High level of market concentration. * Operational performance of the state-owned commercial banks is weak. * The government has been protecting state-owned banks and placing obstacles in the way of foreign banks. * Internal risk controls and appraisal of loan customers are weak.

Opportunities	Threats
* Rising production factor costs are causing transnational corporations to move into China, resulting in increased demand for financing. * The gradual expansion in the number of foreign banks is helping to make the Chinese banking industry more competitive. * Competitive mechanisms are being introduced. * More channels are being created for drawing in foreign capital. * China is getting in line with international practice.	* The market opening which will follow WTO accession will lead to increased competition from foreign banks. * The market share held by foreign banks will gradually increase. * Chinese banks will see their level of operational risk rise. * The difficulty of financial oversight will increase.

3.2 THE INSURANCE INDUSTRY

Beginning in 1980, as foreign insurance companies were allowed to establish representative offices in China, over the next eight years, sixteen American, British and Japanese insurance companies set up representative offices in China. In September 1992, the American insurance company You Bang was granted permission to establish a branch in Shanghai; You Bang is a wholly owned subsidiary of AIG, specializing in life insurance. In July 1994, Tokio Marine and Fire established a Shanghai branch, and in 1995, the list of cities where foreign insurance companies were allowed to set up branches was expanded to include not only Shanghai, but also Guangzhou.

The opening up of the Chinese insurance market to foreign companies nevertheless remains limited and foreign companies wishing to move into the Chinese market have to satisfy several qualifications. They must have been in existence for at least 30 years, must have capitalization of at least US$5 billion, and must have had a representative office in China for at least two years. As of the end of 2001, there were 20 branches of foreign insurance companies operating in China; however, the cities where they could operate were still limited to Shanghai and Guangzhou. In addition to this geographical restriction, those foreign insurance companies which had moved into China were also restricted in their scope of operations.

Casualty insurance companies were only permitted to provide service to foreign companies operating in China, and there were certain types of insurance business which foreign companies were prohibited by law from engaging in, including vehicle and third-party insurance, employer's liability insurance, underwriting loss insurance, import/export product liability insurance, and so on. In addition, they were only allowed to sell property insurance to foreign companies. Foreign life insurance companies were permitted to conduct only individual life insurance business, not group insurance business. Furthermore, since 1996, foreign companies conducting life insurance business in China have been required to do so through joint venture companies; wholly owned companies have not been permitted (Jiao, 2000).

WTO accession is bound to mean further opening of the Chinese insurance market. The main undertakings which China has made in its WTO pre-accession agreements are listed in Table 3.7, while the bilateral agreements made between China and the USA, with regard to the opening up of the insurance market, were as follows (Liu, 2000): (i) geographical restrictions – within five years the geographical restrictions on foreign casualty and accident insurance companies would be lifted, these companies would be allowed to operate in all major cities within two to three years; (ii) scope of business – within five years the scope of permitted business for foreign insurance companies would be expanded to include group insurance, health insurance and endowment insurance (these categories of insurance account for 85 percent of total insurance industry profits); (iii) quantity restrictions – licenses would be awarded in accordance with the principle of caution. Economic considerations would not affect the issuing of licenses, and there would be no quantity restrictions; (iv) equity restrictions – foreign life insurance companies would be allowed to hold a 50 percent share in their Chinese subsidiaries, gradually increasing to 51 percent (i.e. a controlling equity) within one year. The restrictions on the establishment of branches by foreign insurance companies would gradually be lifted. Foreign insurance companies would be allowed to choose their joint venture partners freely. Non-life insurance companies would be allowed to hold a 51 percent share in their Chinese subsidiaries; wholly owned subsidiaries would be permitted within two years; and (v) reinsurance – the reinsurance sector would be opened up completely, with the abolition of all restrictions.

If the contents of Table 3.7 are compared with the bilateral agreements reached between China and the USA, it can be seen that while the undertakings made with respect to quantity restrictions, equity restrictions and the reinsurance sector are more or less the same, with respect to geographical restrictions and scope of business restrictions, China's final undertakings are more sweeping than those made in the bilateral agreements with the USA.

Now that China has joined the WTO, foreign insurance companies are moving into China at an unprecedented speed. In accordance with the pre-accession agreement and the relevant laws and statutes, in early 2003 the China Insurance Regulatory Commission gave its approval for Britain's GAB Robins Group to establish a wholly owned subsidiary in China; previously, in early November 2002, approval had been given for the establishment of branches in China by Britain's Standard Life, US insurance company Li Bao, and Nippon Fire & Marine Insurance of Japan. In early 2002 authorization had been given to Munich Reinsurance Company, Swiss Reinsurance Company and Xin Nuo Insurance of the USA to establish operations in China. This followed the decision in September 2001 to approve the extension of existing China operations by eight foreign insurance companies including Germany's An Lien and Britain's CGU. In the period immediately before and after WTO accession, the USA International Group secured four licenses to establish branches in Beijing, Suzhou, Dongguan (Guangdong Province) and Jiangmen (Guangdong Province); New York Life, Metropolitan and Nippon Life all received permission to establish joint venture life insurance companies in China; Zhong Hong Life Insurance, China's first joint venture insurance company, was granted permission to establish a branch in Guangzhou; Tokio Marine & Fire Insurance was given permission to establish a branch in Shanghai. Foreign insurance companies continued to look for joint venture partners in China, and to undertake preparations for the commencement of operations in China. For example, AEGON Life Insurance of the Netherlands is establishing a joint venture life insurance company in China in collaboration with China Maritime Petroleum; a name – Hai Kang Life Insurance – was recently chosen for this new joint venture company. However, at a time when foreign insurance companies are rushing to move into the Chinese market, some foreign companies which had already established operations in China are actually withdrawing from the market; these include Germany's Koning Insurance, Swiss Life Insurance and the Lincoln Group of the USA.

Table 3.7 WTO Pre-accession Agreement Undertakings within China's Insurance Industry

Current Obstacles and Regulations		Future Market Entry Qualifications
Insurance Industry as a Whole	* The number of foreign insurance companies permitted to operate in China does not exceed 20. Both geographical region of operations and scope of operations are strictly regulated. * Foreign insurance companies are only permitted to operate in Shanghai and Guangzhou; however, AIG has branches in Shenzhen and Foshan. * Only one branch may be established per city.	* Licenses will be issued according to the review standards. Foreign insurance companies must have been operating in a WTO member nation for at least 30 years, must have had a representative office in China for at least two years, and must have (global) capitalization of at least US$5 billion. At the time of WTO accession the minimum asset requirement will be US$500 million; within four years after accession this figure will be gradually reduced to US$200 million. * Following WTO accession, foreign insurance companies and insurance agents will be allowed to provide service in Shanghai, Guangzhou, Dalian, Shenzhen and Foshan. Within two years after accession, the areas within which they are allowed to operate will be expanded to include Beijing, Chengdu, Chongqing, Fuzhou, Suzhou, Xiamen, Ningbo, Shenyang, Wuhan and Tianjin. Within three years after accession, all geographical restrictions will be lifted. * As the geographical restrictions are gradually lifted, foreign insurance companies will be allowed to establish branches in the areas in question.

Table 3.7 Continued

Current Obstacles and Regulations		Future Market Entry Qualifications
Non-life Insurance	* Foreign non-life insurance companies may establish branches, but their customers must be foreign companies. Foreign insurance companies may not undertake car insurance business.	* Following WTO accession, foreign non-life insurance companies will be allowed to establish branches, or joint ventures where the foreign partner's share may be up to 51 percent. The establishment of wholly owned subsidiaries will be permitted within two years after accession. * Following WTO accession, foreign insurance companies will be allowed to provide general policy and/or large-scale commercial risk insurance, without being subject to geographical restrictions. Foreign insurance companies will also be allowed to provide offshore enterprise insurance, foreign enterprise casualty insurance, liability insurance and credit insurance within the geographical restrictions noted in the 'Insurance Industry as a Whole' section above. * Within two years after WTO accession, foreign insurance companies will be allowed to provide the full range of casualty insurance services to both foreign and Chinese customers within the geographical restrictions noted in the 'Insurance Industry as a Whole' section above. * Foreign brokerage firms are permitted to engage in cross-border operations in China or to establish branches in China, to engage in large-scale commercial insurance brokerage business, international sea transport, air transport and road transport insurance business and reinsurance brokerage business.

Table 3.7 Continued

	Current Obstacles and Regulations	Future Market Entry Qualifications
Non-life Insurance		* Foreign non-life companies are permitted to engage in cross-border operations with respect to international sea transport, air transport and road transport insurance business and reinsurance business.
Life Insurance	* The establishment of wholly owned subsidiaries by foreign life insurance companies is permitted, but only under special circumstances. Since 1997, only the establishment of joint ventures has been permitted. Foreign life insurance companies are allowed to conduct only personal life insurance business, not group insurance business.	* Following WTO accession, foreign life insurance companies will be allowed to establish joint ventures where the foreign partner's share may be up to 50 percent. * On the basis of the regulations regarding geographical restrictions noted above, foreign insurance companies will be permitted to provide personal insurance products to both foreign and Chinese customers. Within three years after accession, they will be permitted to conduct medical insurance, group insurance and endowment insurance business.
Reinsurance	* Foreign reinsurance companies are not permitted to conduct RMB business. * Property and accident insurance companies must give 20 percent of their reinsurance business to Chinese reinsurance companies.	* Following WTO accession, there will be no geographical restrictions or quantity restrictions, and foreign insurance companies will be permitted to provide reinsurance services either through branches, joint ventures or wholly owned subsidiaries. * Within four years of accession, the requirement that 20 percent of reinsurance business be given to a Chinese reinsurance company will be abolished.

Source: *Jingji Daobao* (14 January 2002).

Over the period from 2001 to September 2002, twenty-two foreign insurance companies closed a total of thirty representative offices in China (*Zhong Yin Wang*, 22 January 2003). As of the end of 2002, a total of thirty-four foreign insurance companies from twelve different countries and regions had received approval to establish fifty-four branches and offices in China; in more than 40 percent of cases, approval was received after September 2001. The areas in which foreign insurance companies were permitted to do business included the Yangtze Delta (Shanghai), the Pearl River Delta (Guangzhou, Shenzhen, Foshan and Haikou), and North China (Beijing,[4] Tianjin[5] and Dalian[6]) (*Renmin Ribao*, 4 November 2002; *Guoji Jinrong Bao*, 20 December 2002; *Zhong Yin Wang*, 24 January 2003).

As for reinsurance, in October 2002 the China Insurance Regulatory Commission announced changes in the legally required reinsurance ratio. Beginning on 1 January 2003, the ratio was gradually reduced, and eventually legally required ceding will be abolished. The world's two largest reinsurers – Munich Reinsurance and Swiss Reinsurance – have both received permission to establish branches in China (*Zhong Yin Wang*, 13 February 2003).

The strategies adopted by foreign insurance companies for establishing themselves in the Chinese market vary. Some companies enter the market indirectly, by acquiring a share in a Chinese insurance company. Examples include Feng Tai of Switzerland, which holds a share in Tai Kang Life Insurance, Zurich Insurance of Switzerland, which holds a share in Xin Hua Life Insurance, and the ACE Group of the USA, which is Hua Tai's largest shareholder.[7] The HSBC Group is Ping An's third largest foreign shareholder after Morgan Stanley and Goldman Sachs;[8] Citibank has acquired a share in China Life. Other foreign insurance companies have collaborated with leading Chinese firms in other industries. Examples here include the collaboration between New York Life and Haier, between Zhong Li of Italy and China Petroleum, and between AEGON of the Netherlands and China Maritime Petroleum. The Yi An Insurance Group of the USA has joined forces with China Grain, Oil and Food Import/Export Company to establish China's first joint venture insurance brokerage firm (with both parties having a 50 percent share). Since the first half of 2002, those joint venture companies which were already in existence have been increasing their registered capital; both Pacific Aetna and Prudential (Xin Cheng) have increased their capitalization to RMB500 million. Establishing a joint venture with a Chinese company in another industry helps to prevent competition between the joint venture and the Chinese shareholder. In addition, this kind of joint venture allows the foreign partner to exercise effective control over operations, making it less likely that conflict will develop over operational strategy and methods (*Shichang Bao*, 19 December 2002; *Zhong Yin Wang*, 14 January 2003, 22 January 2003).

The overall impact of WTO accession on China's insurance industry will be as follows (Luan, 1998; Shen, 2000; Liu, 2000).

1. *Potential for falling market share of Chinese insurance companies*: Foreign insurance companies have the advantage over Chinese insurance companies in terms of capital, technology, talent, products and scale of operations. Following WTO accession, as the geographical and scope of business restrictions on foreign insurance companies are relaxed, the market share held by the foreign insurance companies will rise. At the same time, the opening up of the car insurance market will, in the short term, cause insurance companies' operating costs to rise, and this will have a direct impact on their profits. In addition, the terrorist attacks on the USA on 11 September 2001 have caused upheavals in the reinsurance market, making it more difficult to secure reinsurance for some important business areas; this will affect insurance companies' ability to take on new business and their financial status (*Jingji Ribao*, 15 January 2002).

2. *The superior fund utilization capability of foreign insurance companies*: Since most foreign insurance companies are transnational business groups, through their careful asset management and fund utilization, they are able to secure high profits from the premium income they receive in the Chinese market. This is why they are able to keep their premium rates so low without affecting their earning ability. At the same time, the different industries in China's financial sector remain separated from one another. The main investment channels for insurance company funds are government bonds and bank deposits, which means that profits are limited, and which puts Chinese insurance companies at a disadvantage since competition is based on premium rates. The ways in which Chinese and foreign insurance companies invest their funds are shown in Table 3.8.

3. *Increasing difficulty of insurance industry supervision*: The competitive mechanism in the Chinese insurance market is not completely sound. Most insurance is provided by state-owned insurance companies, and insurance company management mechanisms need improvement. In addition, in insurance industry regulation, the emphasis is on price and policy terms; there is insufficient concern with solvency and other aspects of operational performance. Furthermore, the legal framework is inadequate. As more foreign insurance groups enter the Chinese market, effective regulation of the industry will become even difficult to achieve.

Table 3.8 Comparison of Chinese and Foreign Insurance Company Investment Channels

Item	Advanced Nations	China
Investment strategy	Securities → real estate → loans → deposits	Deposits → loans → bonds → real estate
Investment in securities	≧80%	≧10%
Cash and bank deposits	0.5–2%	40–50%
Fund utilization rate	≧85%	≦25%
Return on investment	≧12%	≦6%

Note: All figures are averages.

Source: Luan (1998).

4. *Growing competition to secure talent*: Talented personnel are vital in the insurance industry; however, the overall quality of manpower in the Chinese insurance industry is low, and there is a lack of skilled actuaries and claim handling personnel with practical experience. Following WTO accession, foreign insurance companies will be able to head hunt talent away from Chinese insurance companies with the promise of high salaries.

WTO accession will have the following benefits for the Chinese insurance market (Jiao, 2000; Liu, 2002):

1. *Stimulating the development of the Chinese insurance market*: WTO accession will lead to adjustment of the structure of the Chinese insurance industry, and the transformation of management mechanisms. It will make the industry more competitive, enabling it to cope with the competition from foreign insurance companies. In this respect, therefore, WTO accession will be beneficial to the development of the Chinese insurance market.

2. *Increasing availability of different types of insurance product*: As foreign insurance companies move into China, this is bound to lead to an increase in the number of different products available, for example, investment-linked insurance products are starting to appear; banks are starting to sell life insurance, vehicle insurance and travel insurance; premium rates are being adjusted; the personal accident insurance market and short-term health insurance market are being opened up to casualty insurance companies in

order to satisfy steadily increasing demand, thereby increasing business volume and stimulating the development of the intermediary market.

3. *Development of the international markets*: In accordance with the WTO principle of reciprocity, Chinese companies participating in international insurance markets will not be subject to any form of discrimination. This will help the Chinese companies to develop international business.

4. *Improving management capabilities*: Foreign insurance companies possess advanced techniques and extensive management experience. Chinese insurance companies, which are at present handicapped by complex coverage and claim procedures, will be able to learn from their foreign competitors. This will help the Chinese insurance companies to improve their service quality, and speed up their development.

5. *Improvements in the regulatory mechanisms*: Having now joined the WTO, in order to prevent financial crises in other countries from having a negative impact on the Chinese economy, China will have to strengthen the regulation of its insurance market, with the establishment of various ancillary measures.

6. *Potential for improved collaboration with regulators in other countries*: Most foreign insurance companies are transnational business groups with extensive financial resources. China's insurance industry regulator will need to collaborate more closely with the regulators in other countries in order to achieve effective supervision of foreign insurance companies.

To summarize, it is clear that, following WTO accession, as the internationalization of the financial sector continues, there will be opportunities and challenges for both Chinese insurance companies and foreign insurance companies. In order to gauge the impact of WTO accession on the Chinese insurance industry, we will again make use of a SWOT (strength, weakness, opportunity and threat) analysis.

The strengths enjoyed by the Chinese insurance market include the fact that the economy is undergoing rapid transformation, which is thus stimulating economic development. Since the reform began, China has managed to maintain a high economic growth rate; this economic development is of course proving to be the main source of motive power for the development of the insurance industry. Another important point is that China now has a population of 1.3 billion people; however, families are getting smaller, and the population is aging; during the Ninth Five-year Plan (1996–2000) the number of people retiring reached new heights. Income levels are rising, and the consumption structure is changing, leading to increased demand for insurance.

In 2000, China had insurance deepening of 1.8 percent, and insurance density of RMB127.7 (around US$15). These figures are far lower than the averages for the advanced nations, which are 7.5 percent for insurance deepening and US$387 for insurance density. In 2000 the total bank deposits of China's inhabitants came to RMB6,433.24 billion, while total insurance premium income came to RMB159.59 billion, only 2.48 percent of this figure. This is far lower than the average for other developing nations, at 7 percent, or the average for the advanced nations, at 15 percent. Clearly, awareness of the importance of insurance is very low in China, and the Chinese insurance market has great potential waiting to be unlocked. If the average Chinese used 5 percent of their bank savings to purchase insurance, the market that would be created would be enormous (Yang, Fan, 2000).

The inrush of foreign capital following WTO accession will also increase demand for insurance in China, as will the various major construction projects currently underway in China, including the plans to transport natural gas from Western China to Eastern China and the other elements in the 'Great Western Development' plan, the plan to transport water from South China to North China, and the Three Gorges hydroelectric project (Dai, 2002).

The development of the insurance industry depends not only on the use of advanced techniques and effective management strategies, but also on the cultural environment, society's values, religious belief, educational levels, and popular customs. Chinese consumers and Chinese insurance companies share a common cultural background, making consumers more likely to buy insurance from a domestic insurance company. The near monopoly enjoyed by the Chinese insurance companies operating nationwide, coupled with the restrictions placed on foreign insurance companies (in terms of geographical area of operation and business scope) currently allow the Chinese companies to enjoy monopoly profits. This dominance of the market, coupled with their extensive branch network, gives them a major advantage.

As regards the weaknesses of the Chinese insurance industry, the only investment channels open to insurance company funds are bank deposits and the purchase of government bonds, participation in the inter-banks loan market, purchase and sale of bonds, and indirect investment in the stock market through mutual funds. This limited range of investment channels restricts the sources of profits available to them. At the same time, all Chinese insurance companies are state-owned, with weak corporate governance mechanisms. The Chinese government's policy of protecting the state-owned insurance companies and blocking foreign companies' access to the market has reduced the level of competition. As a result, the Chinese insurance companies are saddled with backward management mechanisms, and fund utilization is inefficient. In addition, interest rates in China are low; thus having large amounts of funds deposited in the bank is bound to have a negative impact on insurance companies' operations. Chinese insurance companies have also displayed a lack of innovation in terms of the introduction of new products. Coverage and claim management techniques are not sufficiently highly developed and a high proportion of Chinese insurance company employees are educated to only senior technical school level or below; in 2000, such people accounted for 40 to 50 percent of all Chinese insurance company employees. Employees also tend to be young (in 2000, employees aged 35 or under accounted for 44 to 79 percent of all insurance company employees) and lacking in professional expertise.

Another weakness is that intermediary institutions are underdeveloped. Apart from agents, the only intermediary institutions in existence are consulting firms; these tend to be very small, and are mostly involved in agency work, having only a very limited intermediary function. The quality of intermediary personnel also varies considerably. Furthermore, premium rates in China are set by the regulator, and tend to be on the high side. Insurance companies are subject to rigorous restrictions in terms of what they can do with their funds; therefore, the bulk of their revenue is derived from premium income. In addition, operating costs are high. All these factors combine to keep premium rates high.

As far as reinsurance is concerned, the Chinese reinsurance market has always been an oligopoly. Only three companies, China Reinsurance Company, Pacific and Ping An, are permitted to conduct reinsurance business. The market is small to start with, and this, coupled with the government's implementation of the system requiring insurance companies to give 20 percent of their reinsurance business to domestic reinsurance companies, has restricted competition and slowed the development of the market. On 10 July 2002 a Swiss reinsurance company received approval from the China Insurance Regulatory Commission to establish a subsidiary in China which would operate nationwide. This shows that foreign reinsurance companies will soon be moving into the market, changing the long-standing situation where the market is monopolized by a handful of Chinese companies (*Shichang Bao*, 16 July 2002).

In the future, transnational corporations will keep moving into the Chinese market as part of their global expansion plans, and this rapid growth will lead to increased demand for insurance. The entry of foreign companies into the market and the adoption of new competitive mechanisms will help to improve management techniques in the Chinese insurance industry, contributing to product innovation and the improvement of service quality, and thus enhancing the overall competitiveness of Chinese insurance companies. Furthermore, the WTO's principle of reciprocity means that insurance markets in other countries will be opened up to Chinese insurance firms. Nevertheless, the low level of development reached by the Chinese insurance market means that Chinese insurance companies are not yet on a par with foreign insurance companies (whether in terms of risk management techniques, general management techniques, product innovation or manpower quality).

Following WTO accession, the entry of professionally managed foreign insurance companies will lead to fiercer competition, and the foreign insurance companies' share of the market will gradually increase. Foreign insurance companies will also be able to lure talented Chinese insurance personnel with high salaries; thus the Chinese insurance companies will find that they are losing their best people. As far as securities industry regulation is concerned, the opening up of the market will lead to greater diversification in terms of insurance products, premium rates and market behavior, thereby making effective regulation increasingly difficult (see Table 3.9).

Table 3.9 SWOT Analysis of the Chinese Insurance Industry

Strengths	Weaknesses
* The Chinese insurance companies operating nationwide dominate the market. * Chinese insurance companies have a branch network covering the whole country. * Cultural identity – consumers prefer to buy insurance from domestic companies.	* There is a shortage of human talent and management expertise. * Insurance company fund utilization is inefficient. * Premium rates are too high. * There is insufficient innovation in terms of new insurance products. * Intermediary institutions are underdeveloped. * The government protects domestic insurance companies and creates obstacles to the entry into the market of foreign insurance companies. * Management mechanisms are outdated. * The reinsurance market is underdeveloped.

Table 3.9 Continued

Opportunities	Threats
* Potential demand for insurance is very large. * WTO accession will help make insurance products more competitive. * WTO accession will lead to the adoption of improved management techniques. * In accordance with the WTO principle of reciprocity, other countries' insurance markets will be opened up to Chinese insurance companies, allowing the Chinese insurance industry to expand overseas.	* Competition in the insurance market will get fiercer. * Foreign insurance companies' market share will increase steadily. * Chinese insurance companies will see their best people leaving to join foreign companies. * Regulation of the insurance industry will become more complex.

NOTES

1. These seventeen banks included the Shanghai Branch of HSBC, the Shanghai Branch of DBS Bank, the Shanghai Branch of Mitsui Sumitomo Bank, the Shanghai Branch of Citibank, the Shanghai Branch of Bank of America, the Shanghai Branch of Overseas-Chinese Banking Corporation, the Shanghai Branch of Bank of Malaya, the Shanghai Branch of International Bank Ningbo, the Shanghai Branch of You Li Bank, the Shanghai Branch of Standard Chartered Bank, the Shanghai Branch of Credit Agricole Indosuez, the Shanghai Branch of Societe Generale, the Shanghai Branch of Credit Lyonnais, the Shanghai Branch of State Bank of Bavaria, the Shanghai Branch of Metropolitan Bank & Trust Company, the Shanghai Branch of Australia and New Zealand Banking Group Limited, and the Shanghai Branch of KBC Bank.
2. Once a customer has opened a foreign currency deposit account with Bank of East Asia, no matter how high or low their balance, there is no minimum handling charge for account operation. However, when residents withdraw funds from their account, they have to pay a handling charge of 0.25 percent; this charge applies to all accounts (*Guoji Jinrong Bao*, 11 April 2002).
3. Citibank makes no handling charge for deposits, but there is a 0.25 percent handling charge for withdrawals; this charge is waived once the account has been open for one year (*Guoji Jinrong Bao*, 11 July 2002).
4. In June 2002 the Beijing Branch of US insurance company You Bang began operations, making You Bang the first foreign insurance company to move into the Beijing market.
5. Guangda Yongming Life Insurance, established as a joint venture between Canada's Yongming Life Insurance and China's Guangda Group, became the first joint venture insurance company to be established in Tianjin.
6. On 16 December 2002 Shouchuang Antai Life Insurance, established as a joint venture between Netherlands Insurance and the Capital Group of Beijing, began selling policies in Dalian, making this the third city in North China to have a foreign insurance presence.
7. In May 2002 three insurance companies forming part of the ACE Group paid US$150 million to acquire a 22.13 percent share in Hua Tai, making ACE one of Hua Tai's largest shareholders.

8. The HSBC Group spent US$600 million to acquire a 10 percent share in Ping An Insurance in October 2002.

4. Empirical Analysis of Market Structure, Behavior and Performance

4.1 THE BANKING INDUSTRY

Review of the Literature

Having discussed the institutional development of the Chinese banking industry, potential risk and management efficiency, we will now review the extant literature relating to the reform of banking system in China. Numerous studies in recent years have analyzed the issues surrounding China's financial reform in an effort to gain an understanding of the process of institutional transition in China. Hsiao (1982), for example, discussed some major institutional changes of the early 1980s relating to banking institutions, banking operations, principles of bank management and the role of interest rates, emphasizing that for a number of reasons, the banking system plays an increasing role in the process of China's transitional economy. First of all, the shift of emphasis from major new investment to the efficient use of existing capital will lead to the reinforcement of control of such capital by the banks. Secondly, many economic activities are no longer controlled by administrative orders; instead they are guided by market forces. Thirdly, the function of the banks as an intermediary between savings and investment will acquire added significance and importance. Fourthly, the system of banks is expanding, as a result of international investments, and thus the sources of bank credit are becoming more abundant.

Zhou and Zhu (1987) described the structure of China's banking system at the end of 1985, while also identifying the following six performance-related problems within the system. Firstly, given the planning tradition and administrative character of commercial banks, it is impossible to exercise effective control over the aggregate money supply through partial reserve rates, rediscount rates, open market operations and other instruments of the market mechanism. Secondly, because of the absence of a comprehensive set of effective instruments for parametric macroeconomic regulation, the loan agents are unlikely to implement a loan structure or investment structure which is consistent with social welfare. Thirdly, local governments, at every level, often seriously intervene in the business of commercial bank branches, investment bank branches, and even the local branches of the PBC.

Fourthly, the central government often intervenes in the PBC monetary policies. Fifthly, financial institutions in China run their business based on the principle of operational specialization and monopolistic division. Finally, the interest rate is not sufficiently flexible and does not properly reflect the cost of capital.

In their analysis of the performance of the banking system, Zhou and Zhu also posited three behavioral assumptions: (i) that the State Council and the PBC respond to indications of aggregate excess demand with a time lag; (ii) that local governments intervene less when money is loose than when money is tight; (iii) that bank branches and loan agents make decisions autonomously. A multi-sector general-purpose policy model revealed that the Chinese banking system will characteristically generate a monetary policy cycle between tight and loose money policies, with their results also demonstrating that if banks in China are charged with the dual responsibility of controlling aggregate demand and sector structure, this would create the problems of a business cycle and inefficiency.

Chen (1989) utilized the classical doctrine of the quantity theory of money MV = PQ, where M is the quantity of money in circulation, V is the income velocity of circulation of money, P is the target price level of final output, and Q is the planned final output. The Chinese central authorities set monetary growth to maintain price stability, thus making money supply endogenous in China. Chen focused on the impact of the money supply on China's macroeconomy, examining causal relationships between three alternative monetary aggregates (M0, M2, and M3) and four indicators of macroeconomic performance, namely, economic development, the budget deficit, the trade deficit, and price stability, for the sample period 1951–1985. Chen adopted a Bayesian vector auto-regression model (BVAR), an approach which is 'atheoretical' in the sense that it makes no attempt to use economic theory to impose any a priori restrictions upon the interactions of variables. Chen's empirical results of the five-variable BVAR causality test suggest that the bi-directional causality (feedback) is from the narrowest monetary aggregate (M0) to overall economic development, to the budget deficit, and to the trade deficit, whilst the unidirectional (one-way) causality goes from the money supply to total inflation. Chen further concluded that the most narrowly defined money supply, M0, in particular, reflects the behavior of central authorities as the best target for monetary policy in China's transitional economy.

Bowles and White (1989) utilized Kornai's conceptual framework for the analysis of socialist economies as a means of investigating the extent to which institutional changes in the banking system, since 1984, have created a context for behavioral changes in both banks and enterprises. Kornai's soft budget constraint enabled enterprises to continue to operate, despite making losses and despite demonstrating a high degree of X-inefficiency. Negotiability of tax rates, soft subsidies, soft administrative prices and soft credit are all contributory sources of an enterprise's soft budget constraints, and it is soft credit that is relevant to the analysis of China's banking reform. The banking system has been unable to harden enterprises' credit constraints by increasing the autonomy and commercial orientation of the banks; however, the banks have used their new found powers to expand the volume of credit, fueled by the continuing fund hunger of the still non-restructured state enterprises and the ambitious spending plans of local government. While in theory, banks are empowered to restrict credit to loss-making enterprises and to require them to restructure, this is rarely undertaken in practice; banks usually continue to lend to loss-making enterprises and may try to help them restore their profitability. Bowles and White recognized that as the budget constraints on enterprises have been relaxed through the proliferation of financial institutions and the introduction of various profit retention schemes, the constraints have become softer and directly opposed to the stated aims of the reforms. They conclude that in practice, banking reforms have not led to any significant hardening of credit constraints or changes in enterprises' behavior, indeed, the problems may have become worse.

Hafer and Kutan (1993) considered that financial reform in China had increased the potential importance of monetary aggregates in policy-setting, they therefore investigated the link between both narrow (M0) and broad (M2) monetary aggregates and economic activity in China for the period 1952–1987. The first step in their empirical investigation was to test all data for unit roots by using the Dickey and Fuller procedure, and then to test for the existence of unique cointegrating money, output and prices using the Johansen and Juselius multivariate test procedures. These procedures provide a firmer econometric basis upon which to analyze the issue of selecting appropriate monetary aggregate. Their results indicate that when the retail price index (RPI) is used, feedback exists between M0 and prices, but substituting the implicit national income deflator for RPI results in unidirectional causation running from M0 to prices. Using RPI results in feedback between M2 and prices, and substituting the implicit national income deflator results in unidirectional causation from M2 to prices, they found that monetary measures are not exogenous with respect to output. Since the long-run behavior of prices is directly related to movements in the money stock, both M0 and M2 provide useful information in setting policy. The policy implication of their results on China's transitional economy is that both M0 and M2 must be considered in a monetary policy target.

Yusuf (1994) indicated that China's monetary management seems to have been surprisingly effective in the 1980s; the Chinese policy makers responded to a steady decline in velocity from about 2.5 in 1980, to less than 1 in 1992, by permitting higher rates of credit expansion. The following four key factors are likely to influence the current and future role of monetary policy. Firstly, as direct government subsidies to the SOEs decline, the SOEs become more dependent on financing from banks and financial markets. Secondly, as decentralization has proceeded, the allocation of credit is determined by political bargaining. Thirdly, China is become a more monetized economy. Fourthly, China has promoted a willingness to hold assets in monetary form by adopting a relatively non-repressive interest rate policy.

Ma (1995) presented a game theoretical model to explain that China's inflation over the past decade may have been the result of its decentralized financial system. The basic assumption of the model was that each region has an objective of maximizing local output value, and that credit expansion will be the main method of achieving this goal. The signals that the region uses to choose investment projects are distorted because of price controls in some sectors, while the central government appraises different projects using shadow prices based upon its concerns for economic growth, as well as low inflation. In a scenario of decentralized financial institutions, a game is played between local banks and the central bank which results in equilibrium with inflation. The fundamental source of high output and high inflation is the conflict of interest between central and local governments; this arises because the central government assesses investment projects exerting shadow prices, while the regions count the projects using real prices. Hence, in order to induce a higher credit ceiling from the central bank, the local banks purposely under-invest in the central government's priority projects. In the absence of a mechanism capable of guaranteeing the central bank's commitment to the previously announced credit ceiling, the central bank will have to revise the ceiling upwards, thus creating inflation. Ma's findings proposed that increased central bank independence, further price liberalization, the separation of policy lending from commercial lending, and the separation of local banks from local governments are important policy implications for future financial reform in China.

Lin (1995) noted that a key feature of institutional reform has been the monetization of a previously physically based Chinese planned economy, arguing that rapid and sustained growth in the money supply has been the cause a number of macroeconomic management problems, the first of which was the Chinese government's appropriation of an annual sum corresponding to around 4–5 percent of GDP in reserve money as a means of financing a rising consolidated government deficit (1978–1992). Secondly, China's reformed central bank system (the PBC) suffers from organizational weaknesses; in addition to its lack of policy independence, the heads of the local PBC branches are subservient to the local governments that appoint them, thus the first priority for a local PBC branch head is to accommodate the investment hunger of local governments. Thirdly, administrative instruments of monetary policy, such as direct controls over credit, and indirect instruments, in the form of interest rates and reserve requirements, are weakened by the soft-budget constraints of SOEs and very high household savings pumped into the banking system. Fourthly, financial broadening and innovations have significantly increased intermediation outside the state banking system and the credit plan. Weak supervision of non-bank financial institutions has resulted in their rapid growth in numbers as a means for state banks to engage in unorthodox lending operations, using funds that would otherwise be tied up as excess reserves by the PBC. Lin regarded the root cause of China's macroeconomic instability as a large number of highly inefficient and badly structured SOEs. Unless these are fundamentally reformed, there is no hope of solving the problems of the banking system and persistent fiscal pressures.

Li and Ma (1996) argued that soft-constraint competition is a distinct feature of China's economic fluctuations in the post-reform period; that is, to enhance income and employment levels in their own localities of units, regions and subunits in the state-owned economy scramble for scarce resources. Consequently, investment demand and consumption demand tend to expand, which in turn causes the economy to overheat. Since local banks are under the jurisdiction of local governments, the local governments therefore possess the de facto right to the money supply. They developed a two-region theoretical game model to analyze the impact on local government's investment competition of their de facto right to the money supply in the course of financial liberalization. They assume there are two regions, both of which intend to make investments of desired volumes, which would maximize each region's welfare, and any investment larger or smaller than the desired level would decrease welfare. With the de facto right to the money supply, each region possesses an instrument, such as investment loans from local banks, which is subject to its considerable influence, and the cooperative game minimizes a joint loss function with the regions working together. Their theoretical model showed that monetary decentralization has been a major cause of excessive fiscal deficits and shortages, price liberalization will call for great risk of open inflation, and that the indirect instruments of monetary policy, such as interest rates and reserve requirements, cannot restrict soft-constraint competition. They suggested that ongoing financial reform will push the investment drive by local governments towards the indirect instrument of monetary policy, and that as long as non-cooperative investment competition continues among regions, economic reforms will not be able to avoid the vicious circle of decentralization–recentralization.

There has been a significant increase in the financial deepening ratio of broad money (M2) to GDP in China, from 71.8 percent in 1988, to 107.1 percent in 1994; thus the process of China's financial deepening has been extremely rapid and, since setting out on its institutional reforms, China's economy has become dependent on monetization. The evolution, in rural areas, of the household responsibility system and the emergence of non-state enterprises, such as self-employed, private business and township-village enterprises, are the main reasons for rapid monetization (Girardin, 1997).

Wei and Wang (1997) investigated the issue of lending behavior, and whether state-owned banks have a systematic bias in favor of SOEs. Utilizing data from 370 cities in 1986, 1989, 1990 and 1991, their empirical results did indeed indicate that such a strong bias was present in the lending policies of China's state-owned banking sector, thus cities with a higher SOE share of output are more likely to display faster loan growth. The effectiveness of fiscal and other reforms depends, inversely, on the degree of bank lending bias in favor of SOEs. The policy implication from their analysis is that the reform of the banking sector should be undertaken in conjunction with the reform of SOEs.

Yu (1997) revealed that China's economy has experienced four episodes of Party/Congress-led fluctuations, in 1977, 1982, 1987 and 1992. He conducted unit root and cointegration tests to examine the effectiveness of monetary policy in China, using monthly data for estimation from December 1983 to May 1994. Yu's empirical results showed that tight monetary policy, reinforced by administrative actions, curbs economic heating, and that monetary policy significantly affects industrial output, real sales and prices, but has no effect on fixed asset investment and merchandise imports. He also demonstrated that a long-term, stable relationship exists between financial variables and economic activity, and that monetary aggregates outperform bank credits in predicting future changes in activities. The measurement of monetary aggregates includes M0 (currency in circulation), M1 (currency plus institutional checkable deposits), and M2 (currency plus overall deposits). Yu concluded that since monetary aggregates outperform bank credit in forecasting future economic fluctuations, the PBC is correct in replacing bank credit with monetary aggregates as a major policy target and in switching from direct control of the bank credit to indirect management of monetary aggregates.

Fung et al. (2000) asserted that the Chinese economy differs significantly from the developed economies in two ways. One is its dual structure, comprising a state and a non-state sector; the other is that the financial sector is still monopolized by the government and the state banking system provided for a quasi-fiscal institution. They incorporate these major institutional features of the Chinese transitional economy into an overlapping generation endogenous growth model to investigate the long-run effects of tightening bank credit and raising interest rates on government bonds, bank deposits and bank loans on the expansion of the non-state sector, on the growth rates of output and money supply, and on inflation. Their findings indicate that monetary policy instruments can affect the Chinese economy in the long run in a number of ways. Firstly, raising interest rates on government bonds reduces the inflation rate without tempering the output growth rate. Secondly, reducing bank loans currently available to the state-owned enterprises may lower both the inflation rate and the output growth rate. Thirdly, increasing the nominal interest rate on bank deposits will introduce a stagflationary effect into the economy, such as increasing the inflation rate but reducing the output growth rate. Finally, they noted that changing the nominal interest rate on bank loans will have little real effect.

Wei and Wang (2000) utilized the Data Envelopment Analysis (DEA) method, taking as their sample twelve banks operating in China in 1997 (the Industrial and Commercial Bank of China, the Agricultural Bank of China, the Bank of China, China Construction Bank, the Bank of Communication, CITIC Industrial Bank, China Everbright Bank, China Investment Bank, Guangdong Development Bank, Shenzhen Development Bank, Hua Xia Bank and China Minsheng Bank). They conducted analysis of technical efficiency, pure technical efficiency, scale efficiency and returns to scale, with their results showing that only five banks possessed technical efficiency, and that within this group of five, the Industrial and Commercial Bank of China was the only one of the big four state-owned commercial banks; the other four banks were all new commercial banks, the Bank of Communication, CITIC Industrial Bank, China Everbright Bank and China Minsheng Bank. They also demonstrated that the technical inefficiency of Chinese banks often derives from pure technical inefficiency; this is particularly true of the big-four state-owned commercial banks, whereas with the new commercial banks, technical inefficiency is more likely to derive from scale inefficiency. Furthermore, with the exception of the Industrial and Commercial Bank of China, the other three big state-owned commercial banks have all seen their returns to scale fall rapidly. That is to say, given the level of technology in use, the scale of production at these banks is too large. In the case of new commercial banks which demonstrate technical inefficiency, returns to scale have been increasing rapidly, indicating that, given the level of technology in use, these banks could increase their scale of production.

Wang, Zhenshan (2000) examined the deposit expense rate, loan expense rate, asset expense rate and return on assets of Chinese banks in 1995, in order to analyze their scale efficiency. His results showed that Chinese commercial banks' return on assets showed a U-shaped trend. Medium-sized deposit banks (those with deposits in the region of RMB10–200 billion had a return on assets rate of 1.587 percent, almost 2.8 times as high as that of the large-scale deposit banks (those with deposits of over RMB200 billion) and small-scale deposit banks (those with deposits of under RMB10 billion). The banks with the highest scale efficiency were the medium-sized commercial banks with RMB10–200 billion in deposits. Owing to the lack of clarity regarding ownership rights and other factors, the return on assets rate is not really a good reflection of bank efficiency. As far as cost efficiency is concerned, the operating expense rate falls rapidly as the size of deposits increases. In the case of the loan expense rate, this is 0.36 percent lower for medium-sized banks than for small banks and 0.523 percent lower for large banks than for medium banks. Expense rates for large banks are only 67.14 percent those of the small banks, demonstrating a greater level of scale efficiency. By looking at both the cost and efficiency indicators, it can be seen that it is the medium-sized banks which are the most efficient. Park and Sehrt (2001) pointed out that Chinese banks are inefficient as financial intermediary institutions, and that the financial sector reforms of the 1990s have not improved the operational performance of Chinese banks.

Using the cointegration test and Baynesian vector auto-regression (BVAR), Chen (2002) examined the causal relationship between interest rates, savings and income over the period 1952–1999. Chen's empirical results confirm a stable long-run relationship between interest rates, savings and income, and the BVAR causality test also indicated unidirectional causality running from savings to income. To promote capital accumulation, a financial liberalization package including the independent role of the PBC and interest rate liberalization should be carried out as soon as possible.

Moreover, Leung et al. (2003) utilized survival analysis to examine the factors determining the decision of a foreign bank to establish a branch in China for the period 1985 to 1996. Their results indicated that bank size and international diversification have a significant positive impact on the probability of entry.

Description of Empirical Data and Definition of Variables

As the Chinese banking system has evolved, it has changed from a monopoly by one bank, the PBC, to an oligopoly of the big four state-owned commercial banks, and thereafter, to a situation where the state-owned commercial banks, policy banks and share-type commercial banks coexist. There has therefore been a pronounced increase in the number of market participants. According to neo-classical economic theory, if full competition does not exist, then there will be excessive profits, and the closer the market structure approximates to an oligopoly, the higher these excessive profits will be. This means that changing the market structure is a very important factor in changing the operational performance of banks. As more competition is allowed, the existing banks will find themselves facing greater challenges and risk with respect to their marketing environment and marketing strategy. In particular, given the restrictions placed on them, the state-owned commercial banks and policy banks will find themselves under threat, and will see their market share decline.

Now that China has joined the WTO, the competitive threat to these banks will increase; hence, they will need to implement comprehensive operational planning and secure the government's collaboration if they are to succeed in improving their operational performance. However, the separation between ownership and control in the banking industry creates the potential for principal–agent problems, in the shape of conflict between principal (shareholders) and agent (managers). Both principal–agent problems and the impact of government policy can cause banks to become divorced from the ultimate goal of maximizing profits, concentrating instead on security, liquidity or capital adequacy. That is to say, the emphasis in the managers' behavior is on expediency, and profit performance will suffer. In this study, we will use the market structure–conduct–performance analytical framework developed by Scherer (1980) to explore the impact of market structure on Chinese banks' operational performance management (S–P), and the impact of changes in market structure on bank managers' decision-making conduct (expense preference behavior) (S–C).

With regard to the principal–agent problem, we consider whether there is some disparity between managers' expenditure preference behavior and the bank's ultimate objective of maximizing profits; that is to say, whether managers' potential and actual conduct shows no clear correlation with the bank's operational performance.[1] We will thus be looking at the impact of managers' expense preference behavior on bank management (C–P). The aim of this analysis is to fill a gap in the literature by determining whether the S–C–P relationship postulated by Scherer exists in the Chinese banking industry.

This research was originally intended to take as its sample twenty Chinese banks. These included: (i) policy banks: the State Development Bank, the Export–Import Bank and Agriculture Development Bank; (ii) state-owned commercial banks: the Industrial and Commercial Bank of China, the Agricultural Bank of China, the Bank of China and China Construction Bank; (iii) share-type commercial banks: the Bank of Communication, Shanghai Pudong Development Bank, Fujian Development Bank, Yantai Housing Savings Bank, Bengbu Housing Savings Bank, CITIC Industrial Bank, China Everbright Bank, Hua Xia Bank, China Investment Bank, China Minsheng Bank, China Merchants Bank, Guangdong Development Bank, and Shenzhen

Development Bank. However, as comprehensive data are not available for all the share-type commercial banks, in the end it was possible to produce verified data for only five share-type commercial banks; the Bank of Communication, Yantai Housing Savings Bank, CITIC Industrial Bank, Hua Xia Bank and Shenzhen Development Bank. Foreign banks were excluded from the sample because of the lack of available data, the fact that they are subject to restrictions in terms of scope of business and geographical area of operations, and because they account for only a very small proportion of total deposits and loans.

The period covered by the research is 1995–2001, using data from the 1997–2002 editions of the *Almanac of China's Finance and Banking*. As this period includes the Asian financial crisis of 1997, the period has been divided into two sub-periods: 1995–1997, and 1998–2001. By so doing, we hope to determine whether there was any change in the relationship between structure, conduct and performance in the Chinese banking industry after the Asian financial crisis.

The selection and definition of market structure variables, conduct variables and operational performance variables was as follows.

1. *Market structure variables*: In previous research, the selection of market structure variables has varied depending on the objectives and research subject of the researcher (Gilbert, 1984; Smirlock, 1985). For example, market share, company size and size of assets have all been used as market structure variables. For the purposes of this research, given the data available, it was decided that the following market structure variables should be adopted: (i) size of assets, which can be used to evaluate the bank's scale of operations. In theory, once a bank reaches a certain size it can start to benefit from economies of scale, leading to a reduction in risk and increased profits; (ii) deposit market share. Deposits are main source of funds for banks and the foundation for their creation of credit. This indicator can be used to gain an understanding of how successful a bank is in securing the funds it needs for productive activities. In theory, the lower a bank's share of the deposit market, the higher its funding costs and the lower its productivity; and (iii) loan market share. Loans are the main product of a bank, and its main source of profits. Changes in this variable can show a bank's sales status. In theory, the lower the share of the loan market, the worse the bank's sales status, and the more the bank will be forced to cut interest rates to secure a larger share of the market. The concentration ratio (CRn) and Herfindahl index (H index) are used to measure Chinese banks' share of the deposit and loan markets.

2. *Conduct variables*: When senior bank managers are deciding on their strategy, they will select the key factors in terms of advantages,

disadvantages and environment, and then compare the various strategies available until they can decide on the optimal strategy. However, it is very difficult to quantify manager conduct. We have chosen to look at the responses adopted by banks to deal with changes in the market structure environment, including: (i) professionalization. By improving the quality and professionalism of their employees, banks can increase their productivity. For the purposes of this study, professionalism is measured by looking at the number of bank employees educated to junior college level or above; (ii) diversification. This refers to the process whereby banks expand their scale of operations by moving into business areas other than traditional deposit and loan business, thereby achieving the benefits of economies of scale, reducing risk and increasing profits. In this study, diversification is measured using the proportion of operating revenue accounted for by non-interest revenue; and (iii) the varying impact of employee numbers, depending on managers' decision-making. Where management is based on expediency, the low level of competition is likely to result in the unnecessary expansion of salary budgets and other personnel expenses. In Chinese banks, employees' basic pay is usually based on educational level and years of service, with only small differences between employees. What makes the difference is performance-related bonuses. An increase in the number of employees will not necessarily have a direct impact on profits; however, it can be a response to increased in business demand, in which case it does become a source of increased profits. The number of employees is thus used to examine whether bank manager behavior conforms to the expense preference behavior theory.

3. *Operational performance variables*: When considering banks' operational performance, different indicators can be used depending on whether one is emphasizing liquidity, profitability or security. In this study, the limitations of the data mean that we are restricted to using the following profitability indicators: (i) return on assets (ROA) (= net profit before tax/total assets * 100 percent). This indicator represents an overall appraisal of an enterprise's ability to create profits; the higher it is, the more efficient the bank's utilization of funds; (ii) return on equity (ROE) (= net profit before tax/net worth * 100 percent). This indicator represents the profit that the bank obtains from the use of its own capital in operational activities, or in other words, the net profit per RMB of income. The higher this proportion is, the greater the return on investment, and the greater the bank's earning ability; (iii) net profit ratio (= net profit before tax/operating revenue * 100 percent). This indicator represents total operating and non-operating profit as a proportion of operating revenue over a given period of time; in other words, it is an overall measurement of the bank's operational achievements. The higher this value is, the greater the return on investment, and the greater the

bank's earning ability; (iv) average deposits per employee rate (= total deposits/number of employees * 100 percent). This indicator represents the relationship between the number of bank employees and the funds secured by the bank. The higher this value is, the more funds each employee is securing for the bank, on average; and (v) average profits per employee rate (= net profit before tax/number of employees * 100 percent). This indicator represents the relationship between the number of bank employees and the bank's profits. The higher this value is, the more profits each employee is creating, on average.

4. *Testing hypotheses*: As far as assumptions and verification are concerned, because the sample was too small (less than 30), the Spearman Rank Correlation was used for verification. The verification assumptions were, on the basis of the S−C−P framework, as follows:

1. Market structure has no impact on manager conduct (S−C)

1) $H_0{:}\beta_1 = 0$ There is no significant relationship between the size of bank assets and manager conduct.
2) $H_0{:}\beta_2 = 0$ There is no significant relationship between deposit market share and manager conduct.
3) $H_0{:}\beta_3 = 0$ There is no significant relationship between loan market share and manager conduct.

2. Manager conduct has no impact on operational performance (C−P)

1) $H_0{:}\alpha_1 = 0$ There is no significant relationship between professional management and operational performance.
2) $H_0{:}\alpha_2 = 0$ There is no significant relationship between diversification and operational performance.
3) $H_0{:}\alpha_3 = 0$ There is no significant relationship between the number of employees and operational performance.

3. Market structure has no impact on operational performance (S−P)

1) $H_0{:}\gamma_1 = 0$ There is no significant relationship between the size of bank assets and operational performance.
2) $H_0{:}\gamma_2 = 0$ There is no significant relationship between deposit market share and operational performance.
3) $H_0{:}\gamma_3 = 0$ There is no significant relationship between loan market share and operational performance.

Empirical Results

Analysis of market structure and manager conduct (S–C)

As can be seen from Table 4.1, following the Asian financial crisis in 1997, there was a discernible positive correlation between Chinese banks' total assets and the number of employees, and a negative correlation between total assets and diversification. This indicates that after the Asian financial crisis, Chinese banks saw an increase in both their volume of business and their assets. The number of employees also increased, reflecting an increased emphasis on customer service. This was especially true of the state-owned banks. As the volume of business increased, there was a pronounced trend to become more conservative in managerial strategy, concentrating mainly on traditional deposit and loan business, with banks showing little enthusiasm for diversification into non-traditional business areas. There was no significant correlation between the total assets of state-owned banks and diversification; however, there was a negative correlation between total assets and professionalization. This demonstrates that the increase in employee numbers in the state-owned banks following the Asian financial crisis of 1997 did not represent an increase in professionalization, but rather a simple increase in the number of employees; at the same time, state-owned banks did not show any pronounced enthusiasm for non-traditional deposit and loan business.

In the aftermath of the Asian financial crisis, a positive correlation was discernible between Chinese banks' deposit market share, loan market share and the number of employees. However, there was a negative correlation between loan market share and professionalization. This illustrates that since the Asian financial crisis, an increase in sales was clearly linked to having enough personnel to handle the business, and that Chinese banks are still focusing mainly on developing their traditional deposit and loan business, with no great emphasis on diversification.

There was also a pronounced positive correlation between Chinese banks' deposit market share and the number of employees. Clearly, increased deposit business following the Asian financial crisis was related to having sufficient employees; this was particularly true for the state-owned banks. There was a pronounced negative correlation between state-owned banks' deposit market share and professionalization, indicating that there has been no special emphasis on recruiting personnel with professional expertise during the increase in employee numbers since the crisis. As for policy banks, unlike the state-owned commercial banks, there was a pronounced positive correlation between deposit market share and professionalization, the result showed that policy banks may put much more effort on recruiting personnel with professional expertise since the Asian financial crisis.

Table 4.1 Empirical Results of the Impact of Market Structure on Manager Conduct – Banking

S–C (1998–2001)		All Banks n = 12	State-owned banks n = 3	Policy banks n = 4	Share-type banks n = 5
Size of bank assets has a significant impact on manager conduct	Professionalization		***–		
	Diversification	***–			
	No. of employees	***+	***+		
Loan market share has a significant impact on manager conduct CRn	Diversification	***–			
	No. of employees	***+			
Deposit market share has a significant impact on manager conduct CRn	Professionalization		***–		
	No. of employees	***+	***+		
Loan market share has a significant impact on manager conduct H index	Diversification	***–	***–		
	No. of employees	***+			
Deposit market share has a significant impact on manager conduct H index	Professionalization		***–	***+	
	No. of employees	***+	***+		
S–C (1995–1997)		**All Banks n = 12**	**State-owned banks n = 3**	**Policy banks n = 4**	**Share-type banks n = 5**
Size of bank assets has a significant impact on manager conduct	Diversification			***+	
Loan market share has a significant impact on manager conduct CRn	Diversification			***+	
Deposit market share has a significant impact on manager conduct CRn	Diversification			***+	
Loan market share has a significant impact on manager conduct H index	Diversification			***+	
Deposit market share has a significant impact on manager conduct H index	Diversification			***+	

Notes: *** indicates a significant correlation within a level of significance of 0.5 percent; – indicates a negative correlation; + indicates a positive correlation.

Analysis of manager conduct and operational performance (C–P)

As Table 4.2 shows, after the Asian financial crisis, there was a significant correlation between the increase in the number of bank employees and the increase in professionalization on the one hand, and the average deposits per employee rate and average profits per employee rate on the other. This shows that while increasing the number of employees and enhancing employee professionalism since the Asian financial crisis in 1997, China's banks have been emphasizing customer service, so that the amount of deposits absorbed per employee and the amount of profits created have risen; however, all the state-owned commercial banks have been doing since 1997 is increasing their number of employees, instead of increasing professionalization, not only has earning ability (ROE) not improved, it has actually worsened. This demonstrates that employee professionalism also has to be improved if the aim is to enhance earning ability. Efforts to increase employee numbers and enhance professionalism on the part of the policy banks have caused the average deposits per employee rate to fall. This means that the number of persons employed by the policy banks has already reached uneconomic proportions. With the increase in free competition, the quantity of additional marginal deposits that the policy banks can secure has fallen. In the case of the share-type commercial banks, whereas prior to 1997 diversification had no positive impact on their operational performance, this was no longer true after 1997. This implies that following the Asian financial crisis, and the ongoing opening of China's capital markets, a business model based on diversification is becoming more and more feasible for China's share-type commercial banks. Nevertheless, the diversification of state-owned commercial bank has a negative impact on operational performance

Analysis of market structure and operational performance (S–P)

As can be seen from Table 4.3, there is no significant correlation between Chinese banks' total assets, deposit market share and loan market share on the one hand and their earning ability (ROA, net profit ratio, ROE, average deposits per employee, and so on) on the other. In the state-owned commercial banks, an increase in total assets, deposit market share or loan market share has led to an improvement in earning ability (ROE and average deposits per employee). This shows that the increase in Chinese state-owned banks' traditional deposit and loan business has helped to increase their earning ability.

Table 4.2 Empirical Results of the Impact of Manager Conduct on Operational Performance – Banking

C–P (1998–2001)		All Banks n = 12	State-owned Banks n = 3	Policy Banks n = 4	Share-type Banks n = 5
Professionalization has a significant impact on operational performance.	ROE		***–		
	Average Profits per Employee Rate	***+			***+
	Average Deposits per Employee Rate	***+			***+
Diversification has a significant impact on operational performance.	Average Deposits per Employee Rate		***–		
Number of employees has a significant impact on operational performance	ROE		***+		
	Average Profits per Employee Rate	***+			***+
	Average Deposits per Employee Rate	***+		***–	***+
C–P (1995–1997)		**All Banks n = 12**	**State-owned Banks n = 3**	**Policy Banks n = 4**	**Share-type Banks n = 5**
Diversification has a significant impact on operational performance.	Net Profit Ratio				***–
	ROE				***–

Notes: *** indicates a significant correlation within a level of significance of 0.5 percent; – indicates a negative correlation; + indicates a positive correlation.

Table 4.3 Empirical Results of the Impact of Market Structure on Operational Performance – Banking

S–P (1998–2001)		All Banks n = 12	State-owned Banks n = 3	Policy Banks n = 4	Share-type Banks n = 5
Size of assets has a significant impact on operational performance.	ROA				
	Net Profit Ratio				
	ROE		***+		
	Average Deposits per Employee Rate				
Loan market share has a significant impact on operational performance. CRn	ROA				
	Net Profit Ratio				
	ROE				
	Average Deposits per Employee Rate		***+		
Deposit market share has a significant impact on operational performance. CRn	ROA			***+	
	Net Profit Ratio			***+	
	ROE		***+	***+	
	Average Deposits per Employee Rate				
Loan market share has a significant impact on operational performance. H index	ROA				
	Net Profit Ratio				
	ROE				
	Average Deposits per Employee Rate		***+		
Deposit market share has a significant impact on operational performance. H index	ROA			***+	
	Net Profit Ratio			***+	
	ROE		***+	***+	
	Average Deposits per Employee Rate				
Size of assets has a significant impact on operational performance.	ROA		***–		
	Net Profit Ratio		***–		
	ROE		***–		
Loan market share has a significant impact on operational performance. CRn	ROA		***–		
	Net Profit Ratio		***–		
	ROE		***–		

Table 4.3 Continued

S–P (1995–1997)		All Banks n = 12	State-owned Banks n = 3	Policy Banks n = 4	Share-type Banks n = 5
Deposit market share has a	ROA		***–		
significant impact on	Net Profit Ratio		***–		
operational performance.	ROE		***–		
CRn					
Loan market share has a	ROA		***–		
significant impact on	Net Profit Ratio		***–		
operational performance.	ROE		***–		
H index					
Deposit market share has a	ROA		***–		
significant impact on	Net Profit Ratio		***–		
operational performance.	ROE		***–		
H index					

Notes: *** indicates a significant correlation within a level of significance of 0.5 percent; – indicates a negative correlation; + indicates a positive correlation.

Since 1997, the increase in Chinese policy banks' deposit market share and loan market share has led to a significant increase in earning ability (ROA, net profit ratio and ROE), which indicates that the efforts made by the policy banks since the Asian financial crisis of 1997 to develop their deposit and loan business has improved their earning ability.

To summarize, with the changes in the financial environment and the opening up of the capital markets, the business model adopted by China's banking industry has also changed. For all Chinese banks, traditional deposit and loan business has increased as the market has expanded since the Asian financial crisis, causing average deposits per employee and average profits per employee to increase. Furthermore, as the size of their assets has increased, China's banks have started to pay more attention to customer service, increasing the number of employees. However, the increase in the number of employees has not been accompanied by an increase in professionalism, and no serious efforts have been made to develop new areas of business other than traditional deposit and loan business. Consequently, there has been no significant increase in earning ability.

At the same time, as far as the state-owned banks are concerned, because of the restrictions imposed on them by the government, not only has the increase in the number of employees not led to an improvement in the level of professionalism, it has actually caused it to worsen. In addition, the state-owned banks have not pursued any real effort to develop new areas of business besides their traditional deposit and loan business. Thus the increase in market size has caused average deposits per employee and average profits per employee to increase, and the increase in traditional deposit and loan business has actually improved the state-owned banks' earning ability. This indicates that, because of the near-oligopoly they enjoy, the state-owned banks do remain strong, and they are spending a considerable amount on salaries, but the existence of moral hazard and the high cost of regulation mean that, even if an 'optimal contract' existed, it would not be sufficient to wholly eliminate expediency from manager conduct. As far as the number of employees is concerned, expense preference behavior can be seen. In other words, besides seeking to secure profits, managers may also display risk reduction[2] and expense preference[3] behavior.

4.2 THE INSURANCE INDUSTRY

Description of Empirical Data and Definition of Variables

The institutional evolution of the Chinese insurance industry has seen the industry develop from a monopoly by one company – the People's Insurance Company of China – to a situation where Chinese insurance companies operating nationwide, Chinese insurance companies operating regionally and foreign insurance companies exist side by side; there has thus been a significant increase in the number of market participants.

Leung (2001) used the dynamic general equilibrium model to analyze the relationship between insurance and income distribution, with the results showing that social insurance does not provide an effective solution to inequality in income distribution. Liu et al. (2003) used data from the China Health and Nutrition Survey to test the impact of urbanization on rural health care and insurance; they found that urbanization led to a significant and equitable increase in insurance coverage, which in turn played a critical role in access to care.

As yet, there has been no analysis of the structure of Chinese insurance market. In this study, therefore, we use the structure–conduct–performance analytical framework to analyze the impact of the Chinese insurance industry's market structure on insurance companies' operational performance (S–P), the impact of changes in market structure on insurance companies' decision-making conduct (expense preference behavior) (S–C), and whether it is the case that the managers' decision-making conduct has no significant impact on insurance companies' operational performance (C–P). The aim of this analysis is to determine whether the S–C–P relationship described in Scherer (1980) exists in the Chinese insurance industry.

This research was originally intended to take as its sample twenty-eight insurance companies. These included: (i) Chinese insurance companies operating nationwide: the People's Insurance Company of China, China Life Insurance Company, China Reinsurance Company, Pacific, Ping An, Hua Tai Casualty Insurance Company, Tai Kang Life Insurance Company and Xin Hua Life Insurance Company; (ii) Chinese insurance companies operating regionally: Xinjiang Production Corps Insurance Company, Tian An Casualty Insurance Company, Da Zhong Casualty Insurance Company, Yong An Casualty Insurance Company and Hua An Casualty Insurance Company; (iii) foreign and joint venture insurance companies: Min An (Haikou) (Hong Kong), Min An (Shenzhen) (Hong Kong), AIG (Shanghai) (USA), AIG (Guangzhou) (USA), AIG (Shenzhen) (USA), Mei Ya (Shanghai) (USA), Mei Ya (Guangzhou) (USA), Mei Ya (Shenzhen) (USA), Tokio Marine & Fire (Japan), Zurich (Shanghai) (Switzerland), Zhong Hong Life Insurance, Pacific Aetna Life Insurance, Jin Sheng Life Insurance, An Lian Da Zhong Life Insurance, and Royal Sun (Shanghai). However, because the data available for the foreign and joint venture insurance companies were not sufficiently comprehensive, in the end it was possible to produce verified data for only seven foreign and joint venture insurance companies – AIG (Shanghai) (USA), Min An (Shenzhen) (Hong Kong), Min An (Haikou) (Hong Kong), Zhong Hong Life Insurance, Tokio Marine & Fire, Mei Ya (Shanghai) (USA) and Mei Ya (Guangzhou) (USA).

The period covered by the analysis is 1998–2001, using empirical data from the 1997–2002 editions of the *Almanac of China's Finance and Banking* and the 1999–2002 editions of the *China Insurance Yearbook*. The selection and definition of market structure variables, conduct variables and operational performance variables was as follows.

Market structure variables

In selecting the market structure variables, the authors took into consideration the variables used in prior research and the availability of data. Premium income market share was selected to be able to evaluate insurance companies' scale of operations. As premium income is an insurance company's main source of funds, which it uses to create credit, using this indicator makes it possible to gain an understanding of how insurance companies secure the funds they need for their productive activities in conditions of free competition. In theory, when premium income market share falls, funding costs will rise, and productivity will fall. The concentration ratio (CRn) and Herfindahl index (H index) are used to measure insurance companies' premium income market share.

Conduct variables

When insurance companies' senior managers are making their strategy decision, they will select key factors in terms of advantages, disadvantages and environment, and then compare the various strategies available until they can decide on the optimal strategy. However, it is very difficult to quantify manager conduct. We have chosen to look at the responses adopted by insurance companies to deal with changes in the market structure environment, including: (i) professionalization. By improving the quality and professionalism of their employees, insurance companies can increase their productivity. For the purposes of this study, professionalism is measured by looking at the proportion of insurance company employees educated to junior college level or above; (ii) diversification. This refers to the process whereby insurance companies expand their scale of operations by moving into business areas other than traditional insurance business, thereby achieving the benefits of economies of scale, reducing risk and increasing profits. In this study, diversification is measured using the proportion of operating revenue accounted for by non-premium income; and (iii) the impact of employee numbers varies depending on managers' decision-making. Where management is based on expediency, the low level of competition is likely to result in unnecessary expansion in salary and other personnel expenses. An increase in the number of employees will not necessarily have a direct impact on profits; however, it can be a response to increased demand, in which case it does become a source of increased profits. The number of employees is thus used to examine whether insurance company manager conduct conforms to the expense preference behavior theory.

Operational performance variables

After taking into consideration the limitations of the data which were available for this study it was decided to use the following profitability indicators: (i) return on equity (ROE) (= net profit before tax/net worth * 100 percent). This indicator represents the profit which the insurance company obtains from the use of its own capital in operational activities, or in other words, the net profit per RMB of income. The higher this proportion is, the greater the return on investment, and the greater the insurance company's earning ability; (ii) net profit ratio (= net profit before tax/operating revenue * 100 percent). This indicator represents total operating and non-operating profit as a proportion of operating revenue over a given period of time; in other words, it is an overall measurement of the insurance company's operational achievements. The higher this value is, the greater the return on investment, and the greater the insurance company's earning ability; and (iii) debt ratio (= total liabilities/net worth * 100 percent). This indicator represents borrowed funds as a percentage of own capital. The higher this value is, the more indebted the enterprise is, and the more interest it has to pay.

Testing hypotheses

As far as assumptions and verification are concerned, because the sample was too small (under 30), the Spearman Rank Correlation was used for verification. The testing hypotheses were, on the basis of the S–C–P framework, as follows:

1. Market structure has no impact on manager conduct (S–C)

1) $H_0: \beta_1 = 0$ There is no significant relationship between premium income and manager conduct.

2. Manager conduct has no impact on operational performance (C–P)

1) $H_0: \alpha_1 = 0$ There is no significant relationship between professional management and operational performance.
2) $H_0: \alpha_2 = 0$ There is no significant relationship between diversification and operational performance.
3) $H_0: \alpha_3 = 0$ There is no significant relationship between the number of employees and operational performance.

3. Market structure has no impact on operational performance (S–P)

1) $H_0: \gamma_1 = 0$ There is no significant relationship between premium income and operational performance.

Empirical Results

Analysis of market structure and manager conduct (S–C)

As can be seen from Table 4.4, in the Chinese insurance industry there is a clear positive correlation between premium income market share and the number of employees. This demonstrates that any increase in product sales is closely related to having an adequate number of service personnel; however, for the Chinese insurance companies operating nationwide, there is a clear negative correlation between premium income market share and professionalization. This indicates that the additional employees being recruited to cope with an increasing volume of business do not have a particularly high level of professional expertise; hence, all that is being increased is the number of employees.

Analysis of manager conduct and operational performance (C–P)

As can be seen from Table 4.4, there is a clear positive correlation between the number of employees and the insurance company's debt ratio. This shows that while increasing the number of employees does help to increase product sales, it also increases the company's debt ratio. With regard to foreign insurance companies, since many restrictions placed on foreign and joint venture insurance companies in terms of business areas and region of operation, an increase in the number of employees is unlikely to improve their earning ability (ROE) significantly.

Analysis of market structure and operational performance (S–P)

Table 4.4 also demonstrates a clear positive correlation between premium income market share and the debt ratio, which shows that in Chinese insurance companies an increase in premium income market share leads to an increase in the debt ratio. At the same time, while foreign insurance companies and joint ventures have seen their premium income market share rise, this has not led to any real improvement in their earning ability. This is probably related to the many restrictions placed on foreign and joint venture insurance companies in terms of their business areas and region of operation.

To summarize, in terms of the Chinese insurance industry as a whole, as the market has expanded, insurance companies have begun to pay more attention to customer service in order to increase their market share; this has led them to increase the number of personnel employed. This increase has not, however, been accompanied by an increase in professionalism. At the same time, increased premium income market share has led to an increased debt ratio; it can thus be seen that because of the near-monopoly they enjoy, the Chinese insurance companies operating nationwide remain strong and are spending a considerable amount on salaries, but the existence of moral hazard and the high cost of regulation means that, even if an 'optimal contract' existed, it would not be sufficient to wholly eliminate expediency from manager conduct. With regard to the number of employees, expense preference behavior can be found; besides seeking to secure profits, managers may also reveal risk reduction and expense preference behavior. In addition, owing to the restrictions imposed on foreign and joint venture insurance companies in terms of business areas and region of operation, their increased premium income market share has not helped them to increase their earning ability.

Table 4.4 Empirical Results of the Relationship between Market Structure, Manager Conduct and Operational Performance – Insurance

S–C(1998–2001)		All Insurance Companies n = 20	Chinese Insurance Companies Operating Nationwide n = 8	Chinese Insurance Companies Operating Regionally n = 5	Foreign Insurance Companies n = 7
Premium income has a significant impact on manager conduct CRn	Professionalization				
	No. of employees	***+			***+
Premium income has a significant impact on manager conduct H index	Professionalization		***–		
	No. of employees	***+	***+		
C–P (1998–2001)					
Diversification has a significant impact on operational performance	Debt ratio			***+	
	ROE				
No. of employees has a significant impact on operational performance	Debt ratio	***+			
	ROE				***–
S–P (1998–2001)					
Premium income has a significant impact on operational performance CRn	Debt ratio	***+	***+		
	ROE	***+			***–
Premium income has a significant impact on operational performance H index	Debt ratio	***+			
	ROE				***–

Notes: *** indicates a significant correlation within a level of significance of 0.5 percent; – indicates a negative correlation; + indicates a positive correlation.

NOTES

1. The expenditure preference behavior theory was first put forward by Williamson (1963). Its main contention is that, when there is a lack of competition in the market and an enterprise enjoys some level of monopoly status within its industry, the enterprise's managers will exploit their monopoly power to increase their managerial discretion. Williamson converted non-measurable personal motivation into measurable external behavior. For example, in order to enhance their own position within the company (internal motivation), a manager might arrange for the company to increase employees' salaries (external behavior) so as to win employees' support and confidence. The results of the external behavior can thus be used as an indicator of the extent to which managers have become divorced from the goal of maximizing profits.
2. The risk reduction theory was proposed by Heggestad (1977). It suggests that the higher the level of concentration within the banking industry, the fewer banks will want to hold assets which have a high level of risk.
3. The expense preference theory was put forward by Edwards (1977), who suggested that banks in an area with high market concentration would exploit their control over the market to engage in expense preference behavior, rather than making profit maximization their main motive. The empirical results produced by Qin and Ouyang (2002) show that expense preference behavior does exist among the four big state-owned commercial banks in China.

5. Perspectives

One of the main factors behind China's rapid economic development has been the phenomenally rapid growth within the country's financial sector. China is currently engaged in the process of institutional transformation from a planned economy into a market economy, during which the financial risk inherent in the old system and the risk created by institutional change continue to coexist. With WTO accession and the opening up of the financial services industry to foreign companies, competition will become fiercer, leading to an increase in uncertainty, and thereby making the level of risk even greater. At the same time, the financial markets are becoming increasingly divorced from real economic activity with the rapid flow of capital and the dramatic fluctuations in exchange rates also contributing to the increasing level of risk. The move in and out of the country of large quantities of international capital (particularly short-term capital) tends to make China's financial ups and downs even more dramatic, increasing the level of risk, while there is also the ever-present danger of financial crises spreading from one country to another.

The measures to be adopted by Chinese banks both in response to the challenges presented by WTO accession, and in an effort to prevent future financial crises, can be divided into several categories, including systems, sales, human resources, market operations, liberalization of the financial markets, reform of the legal system, increased transparency, and so on.[1] These are discussed separately below.

Clarification of Property Rights

In order to solve the problem of unclear property rights which currently affects the state-owned banks, China is seeking to speed up the transformation of the state-owned commercial banks into share-type commercial banks by clarifying the rights and obligations of owners, managers and employees. The government also wants to move away from the situation where the government itself is the only investor in the state-owned banks, bringing in other investors to share profits and spread risk. Converting the state-owned commercial banks into share-type banks will also have the advantage of bringing about diversification of ownership, thereby achieving a fundamental solution to the shortage of capital which has long plagued the state-owned commercial banks. The first step in the reform of the state-owned commercial banks is to implement a stock-taking of their assets in order to determine the exact composition of their actual assets and liabilities. Capital increments can then be implemented in accordance with the provisions of the Company Law and the Commercial Banking Law.

If the state were permitted to hold no more than a 50 percent share in the banks, it would be possible to achieve dispersal of equity while still allowing the state to retain the largest share. Once the state-owned commercial banks had established modern governance mechanisms, the state's share could then be gradually reduced. Eventually, those state-owned commercial banks which conformed to requirements could be listed on the stock exchange. There would be a number of advantages gained by converting the state-owned commercial banks into share-type banks. For example, the introduction of new shareholders and new capital would help the banks to reduce their non-performing loan ratios and increase their capital adequacy ratios. It would also mean that the state would simply be the largest shareholder rather than the sole owner of the banks. With the reduction of state control over the banks, the increase in non-performing assets could be brought under control. Reform of the ownership structure would also solve the principal–agent problem, contributing to a strengthening of supervision and providing bank employees more incentives to work harder. The Industrial and Commercial Bank of China is preparing to spend five years sorting out its non-performing loans and strengthening the bank's governance structure, promoting conversion to a share-type commercial bank with the Bank's overall aim being to achieve stock market listing by 2005.

In response to the threat posed by foreign banks, China's state-owned commercial banks have been seeking to reform their corporate governance structures and to develop plans for stock market listing. Bank of China, China Construction Bank and Industrial and Commercial Bank of China have all taken steps in this direction. Currently, only four Chinese banks are listed in China's stock exchanges: Pudong Development Bank, Shenzhen Development bank, Minsheng Bank and China Mechants Bank.

The state banks are also stepping up their collaboration with foreign banks, making use of the services of international management consultancy firms to enhance their competitiveness. The China Minsheng Bank Corporation is to begin collaboration with thirty-two foreign banks, including Citibank, HSBC, Credit Agricole Indosuez, KBC Bank, Bank of Tokyo-Mitsubishi, DBS Bank, Overseas-Chinese Banking Corporation, Bangkok Bank, Mitsui Sumitomo, Societe Generale, Deutsche Bank, ABN AMRO Bank, Bank of America, Netherlands Bank, Credit Lyonnais, Australia and New Zealand Banking Group, Dresden Bank, Intesa Banca Commerciale Italiana, Commerzbank, Hang Seng Bank, International Bank of Thailand, Bank of East Asia, Mizuho

Corporate Bank, Han Hui Bank, Hua Yi Bank, UFJ Bank, Credit Suisse First Boston, Korea Industrial Bank, Shanghai BNP, Bao Sheng Bank, Standard Chartered Bank and Da Tong Bank. The scope of collaboration will include international settlement for foreign currency operations, foreign currency cash operations, foreign currency credit card operations, foreign currency, foreign currency inter-bank loans, RMB inter-bank loans, RMB agency collection and payment, standby letters of credit for RMB payment, syndicated loans, foreign currency swaps, RMB bill discounting, customer surveys and human resources training.

The Adjustment of Commercial Bank Structure and Establishment of Sound Management Mechanisms

There is a need for banks to establish sound management mechanisms, strengthening coordination between different levels and different departments, in order to make a clear separation between policy tasks and commercial activity, to reduce the policy burden on the state-owned commercial banks, to strengthen internal controls, and to reduce government interference. The management of the state-owned commercial banks should be based on commercial principles with the banks enjoying complete autonomy with respect to their loan and investment policy; they should aim to establish sound risk evaluation and monitoring systems in order to facilitate their transformation into modern financial enterprises.

Eliminating Barriers within the Financial Services Industry

At present, in order to prevent cross-subsidization and prevent non-bank financial institutions from using affiliated banks to engage in unfair competition, China's banking industry, insurance industry and securities industry are kept strictly separated from one another; however, having now joined the WTO, China is faced with a situation where this separation harms the international competitiveness of the financial institutions and inhibits innovation within. It also makes it impossible to meet the diverse needs of customers with respect to financial products.

The financial markets are now being opened up, and the restrictions governing bank operation of securities and insurance businesses are being relaxed. The People's Bank of China has relaxed the regulations governing participation in the national inter-bank bond market. All commercial banks operating in China (and their licensed branches), investment and trust companies, business group financial companies, finance and leasing companies, rural credit cooperatives, urban credit cooperatives, securities firms, fund management companies (and the funds they manage), insurance companies, foreign financial institutions, and all other types of financial institution which have been authorized by the authorities to invest in bonds, may participate in the national inter-bank bond market without being required to make a special application for permission to participate.

The trend towards integration of different financial businesses is thus an inevitable one, and the banking industry needs to start planning and accumulating experience in this field as early as possible. At present, the assets and market share held by the share-type commercial banks are far lower than those held by the big four state-owned commercial banks. Mergers between share-type commercial banks would help to expand their scale of operations and increase their competitiveness, making them better able to deal with the increasingly fierce competition in the market.

Development of Traditional Businesses and Financial Innovation

China's banks need to attach greater importance to marketing and to strengthening their relationships with existing customers. Their traditional product-oriented marketing strategy needs to be replaced by a customer-oriented strategy, with new products being constantly launched so as to achieve greater market penetration. The banks need to develop new sources of customers, such as medium-sized corporations with good prospects, and to provide their customers with high quality service, so that they can develop their traditional businesses. The banks also need to develop off-balance-sheet businesses, speed up the process of e-adoption, enhance the efficiency of the service they provide, and strengthen the development of new products. They need to strengthen their ability to innovate, so that they can develop financial products suited to the needs of different types of enterprise and individual, thereby enhancing their competitiveness. At the same time, Chinese banks can make use of the WTO principle of reciprocity to establish branches overseas and develop international markets.

Improving the Quality of Human Resources

Chinese banks need to establish human resources management systems which conform to the needs of a modern commercial bank. They need to strengthen the training of their existing managers, so as to improve their overall quality. WTO accession means constant innovation and fierce competition; there is an urgent need for managers familiar with the international financial system and practice, and the legal framework, plus additional skills in foreign languages and computers. Chinese banks also need to recruit financial talent from overseas, recruiting for example, returning students and employees of foreign financial institutions who have extensive experience and are familiar with how the international financial markets operate. These people are needed not only in the banks themselves, but also in the regulatory agencies. There is also a need for greater international collaboration in the financial sector. Foreign financial experts can be invited to come and teach or hold seminars in China, and middle-ranking and senior managers and technical personnel can be sent overseas for training.

Establishment of a Market Environment Based on Fair Competition

The first priority in establishing a fair market environment is to adjust the government's overall financial policy, with the development of monetary policy suited to an open economy. The PBC needs to be given more autonomy with respect to the formulation of monetary policy, to enhance its overall control and supervision capabilities. As more foreign banks move into China, there will be a need for the establishment of a control system which can achieve effective regulation of the foreign banks and prevent excessively large amounts of capital from moving into or out of the country in a short space of time.

Owing to the separation of the different segments within the financial services industry, at present the PBC, China Securities Regulatory Commission (CSRC) and China Insurance Regulatory Commission (CIRC) all operate independently of one another; clearly, therefore, there is an urgent need for the introduction of a unified regulatory system. Given the trend towards increased integration of the world's financial markets, effective regulation of foreign banks will require collaboration with the regulatory agencies in other countries. Chinese needs to step up its efforts in this particular area if it is to improve the efficiency of regulation at home.

Accelerating the Expansion of the Market Mechanism in Monetary Policy Tools

At present, the market plays only a very limited role in the monetary policy tools used in China. In particular, the part which the market plays in the setting of interest rates is minimal. Interest rate controls distort the allocation of credit, and reduce the ability of commercial banks to avoid interest rate and exchange rate risk; this tends to encourage rent-seeking by both Chinese and foreign banks and makes it more difficult for the PBC to exercise overall supervision over the banking industry.

The controls on interest rates should be abolished, starting with the money market and moving on to loan and deposit interest rates. The RMB exchange rate mechanism also needs to be improved in order to provide increased flexibility and make it a more effective means of both regulating China's international balance of payments and maintaining financial stability. The pursuit of market operations transparency should be an important tool of monetary policy, and yet China has not made any serious efforts to bring about such a change. The number of financial institutions participating in the open market is small, the number and volume of transactions are small, and there is no supervisory committee with sufficient power and influence to regulate market operation. At present, open market operation is regulated by the PBC, and in reality, exists in name only. China needs to speed up the establishment of comprehensive open market operations, in order to ensure that this becomes an effective tool within the application of monetary policy.

Establishing a Proper Legal Framework for the Operations of Foreign Banks

As yet, China lacks a comprehensive legal framework for regulating the operations of foreign banks; thus, in order to strengthen the regulation of foreign banks, the PBC formulated the Statute Governing the Management of Foreign Financial Institutions, which came into effect on 29 December 2001, and the Implementation Regulations for the Statute Governing the Management of Foreign Financial Institutions, which came into effect on 1 February 2002. The Implementation Regulations lay down the requirements for the establishment of a branch in China by a foreign or joint venture bank, which are: (i) the applicant bank must have had a representative office in China for at least two years; and (ii) in the year prior to application its total assets must not have fallen below US$20 billion. As long as these conditions are met, a bank can apply to establish a branch in any city in China. The Implementation Regulations also specify the requirements that have to be met before a bank will be allowed to conduct foreign exchange operations (either a restricted set of foreign exchange operations, or all foreign exchange business), along with other clear requirements for working capital levels for different types of foreign financial institution.

In February 2002, the People's Bank of China promulgated the Management Regulations Governing the Establishment of Branch Networks by Banks in the Same City. The Regulations stated that the decision by the People's Bank of China as to whether banks would be permitted to establish multiple branches in the same city would be based on the need to maintain a reasonable level of competition, the state of development of the banking sector in the area in question, and the need to satisfy local demand for banking services. One point worth noting is that these Management Regulations apply to both Chinese banks and foreign banks, in accordance with the WTO's 'national treatment' principle. According to the Management

Regulations, a commercial bank may only apply to establish a single branch in a given city at a time. Once approval has been given, the bank may then apply to establish another branch. In addition, a commercial bank may not apply to establish more than three 'self-service banks' in a given city at a time. These regulations go some way towards ensuring gradual market entry by foreign banks, and should ensure that the impact of competition from foreign banks on Chinese banks (particularly in major cities) is limited.

In March 2002, the People's Bank of China promulgated the Management Policy Governing Interest Rates on Foreign Currency Deposits and Loans Applying to Chinese and Foreign Financial Institutions; these regulations establish a unified foreign currency interest rate management system applying to both domestic and foreign banks. In July 2001, the Management Regulations Governing Inter-Bank Business was promulgated, creating new possibilities for the development of inter-bank business. The People's Bank of China is currently engaged in formulating management regulations to govern the acquisition of shares in domestic banks by foreign banks, along with automobile financing and consumer loan services.

The PBC is also empowered to make special requirements regarding capital adequacy ratios according to foreign financial institutions' level of risk. China needs to follow international practice by formulating a Foreign Banks Law, Joint Venture Banks Law, Foreign Finance Companies Law, and a Statute Governing the Punishment of Foreign Financial Institutions Violating the Law, in order to regulate market entry, asset levels, capitalization standards, scope of business, internal controls, risk appraisal systems, disclosure and legal violations. In addition, foreign banks could be requested to follow the example of domestic Chinese banks by establishing a banking association for self-regulation.

Providing Reasonable Protection for State-owned Commercial Banks

China should make full use of its status as a developing nation to provide suitable levels of protection for its state-owned commercial banks. The PBC needs to speed up the process of market-determined interest rates, giving the big state-owned commercial banks more freedom to set their own interest rates and the prices of their financial products. That is to say, the state-owned commercial banks need to be given more autonomy, so that they can exercise greater flexibility with respect to interest rates and fees, thereby making it easier for them to compete against foreign banks.

The preferential tax treatment enjoyed by foreign banks should also be abolished, so that the state-owned commercial banks can compete on an equal footing with the foreign banks in this respect. The government also needs to set up an exit mechanism for financial institutions, and to ensure that the necessary laws are enacted for the regulation of mergers and acquisitions between banks. In addition, the reform of the state-owned enterprises needs to proceed simultaneously with the reform of the banking industry, so that synergy can be created between the two.

Gradual Opening Up of the Financial Markets

As a result of WTO accession, the following timetable has been set for financial liberalization. Within three years, the non-performing asset problem affecting state-owned enterprises and state-owned banks will have been solved, thereby enhancing the competitiveness of Chinese banks. Within two to three years, interest rates will have been freed up; however, to avoid overreaction by the market, this will be implemented gradually, starting with money market interest rates, before moving on to loan rates, with deposit rates coming last. Interest rates will then be determined by the market mechanism. Within one year, financial institutions will be able to move into financial sector business areas outside their own particular area. Within three to five years, the RMB will be traded freely and conversion of capital items will be permitted.

Establishment of a Legal System Conforming to International Standards

Although China has begun to establish a much-needed legal framework for the regulation of financial activities, as a result of the major changes occurring in the financial environment, some of the provisions of the People's Bank of China Law, Commercial Banking Law, Insurance Law, Securities Law and the like no longer conform to the needs of the development of the banking industry or to banking industry regulation. For example, the Commercial Banking Law provides insufficient legal protection for the rights of commercial banks and their scope of business is restricted to traditional banking activities, which is not conducive to innovation. There are no clear provisions governing commercial banks' internal governance structure, internal controls or transparency. There is also a lack of clear regulations governing market exit for Chinese and foreign banks.

Now that China has joined the WTO, the need for improvement of the legal environment is even more urgent, particularly with respect to the regulation of the financial sector, telecommunications industry, and so on. China's existing legal system needs to be revised as soon as possible, to include, for example, formulation of a Statute Governing the Bankruptcy of Financial Enterprises so as to provide for market exit. China needs to ensure that its legal system conforms to WTO requirements, establishing new laws, as necessary, in accordance with those requirements.

The People's Bank of China is speeding up the formulation of the Management Regulations Governing Foreign Participation in Chinese Commercial Banks, which will regulate the purchase, transfer and sale of shares in domestic commercial banks by foreign financial institutions. The Bank is also drawing up Management Regulations Governing Participation in Chinese Financial Institutions by Foreign Financial Holding Companies, to provide a basis for comprehensive supervision of foreign financial holding companies operating in China. In addition, Management Regulations Governing the Undertaking of Information Outsourcing Business by Foreign Financial Institutions are being formulated; these will allow small and medium-sized domestic banks to make use of the data processing centers, bill processing centers and operations centers established by foreign commercial banks in China, thereby avoiding duplication of investment.

Increasing the Level of Transparency in the Financial Sector

In order to meet the needs of WTO accession, there should be an increase in the level of transparency of policy-making within the PBC. The government also needs to establish a comprehensive compulsory disclosure system for financial institutions, and to promote the establishment of smooth channels of communication between banks in order to facilitate the sharing of customer credit rating data and prevent customers with doubtful creditworthiness from borrowing simultaneously from multiple banks or from defrauding several banks in a row.

On 24 May 2002, the PBC introduced the Provisional Regulations Governing the Disclosure of Information by Commercial Banks, providing overall regulation of disclosure principles, content, methods and programs, in order to strengthen the self-regulation of commercial banks, regulate the disclosure of information, ensure that the rights of depositors and other interested parties are protected, and promote security, stability and efficiency within the banking industry. The regulations, which apply to Chinese commercial banks, wholly foreign-owned banks, Sino-foreign joint venture banks and the Chinese branches of foreign banks, stipulate that the financial reports issued by commercial banks must be audited by a qualified firm of accountants.

Strengthening Financial Regulation

China can be expected to maintain the barriers which exist between the banking, securities and insurance sectors for some time to come. Concrete measures which have been taken to strengthen regulation of commercial banks include the following. On 1 January 2002, the government implemented a new management system whereby all loans made by commercial banks in China are graded on a five-classification (mention, pass, special mention, substandard, doubtful and loss). Systems for bad debt reserve and bad debt write-off are being established in accordance with regular international practice. New auditing and accounting systems are being introduced. All commercial banks are being required to bring their capital adequacy ratios up to the level required by law within a specified time limit, and supplementary capitalization is to be permitted.

Furthermore, China established a new regulatory body (China Banking Regulatory Commission) to oversee banking regulations and strengthen supervision in March 2003.

Developing Off-balance-sheet Business

Off-balance-sheet business is a bank's main source of service charge income; it is also an important means for building up its customer base. It is important for banks to gain an understanding of what society needs in the way of intermediary services, so that they can develop the relevant businesses. Banks in China are starting to insist that all their branches work to develop intermediary businesses such as negotiation of documentary bills, credit card business, safety deposit box business, consulting services, leasing, insurance agency, securities repurchase and discretionary trading. Banks are also working to improve the efficiency of the service they provide in intermediary businesses, focusing on overall improvement to attract more new customers.

Seeking New Breakthroughs for Banking Business in the Capital Markets

Banks are stepping up their collaboration with securities firms, and seeking to develop bank off-balance-sheet business in the securities market. They have been aggressively developing securities pledge loans, and working together with securities firms to develop inter-bank loan and government bond repurchase business. Banks are also starting to undertake the issuing and underwriting of government bonds on an agency basis, along with the issuing of corporate bonds. Banks are also making use of the opportunities presented by stock market listing to improve their customer base through the selection of appropriate shareholders and medium/long-term strategic investors.

Aggressive Development of New Business Areas

One new business area which banks in China are developing is leasing business. The risk in leasing business is relatively easy to control, and it offers a steady revenue stream. Despite these advantages, this is one of the areas where Chinese banks are weakest. Commercial banks are at an advantage over ordinary leasing companies when it comes to the development of leasing business, with their easy access to funds and to different sources of information. In particular, commercial banks have an in-depth understanding of their customers' financial status; they can leverage this knowledge in the development of their leasing business.

Another new business area which offers great potential is consulting services. Banks can leverage their advantages in terms of information and manpower resources to develop consulting services (for both corporate and individual clients) in the areas of asset management, debt management, risk management, liquidity management, investment portfolio design, household financial planning, appraisal, etc. Banks are starting to establish information management and consulting centers, in an extension of the functions of their existing settlement and agency centers. They are also developing new on-line services to enhance their competitiveness.

The strategies which will be utilized by the Chinese insurance industry in response to WTO accession include the following.[2]

Speeding Up of Systemic Reform in the Insurance Industry and Establishing Comprehensive Management Mechanisms

The lack of effective management mechanisms is one of the main factors responsible for lowering the competitiveness of the Chinese insurance industry. The state-owned insurance companies need to be converted to share-type companies, with the establishment of first-class governance structures and comprehensive management mechanisms. Insurance companies should also be permitted to raise funds from the capital markets, to ease their problem of capital shortage. The fund utilization of the Chinese insurance industry also needs to be improved to enable insurance companies to access the capital markets. As well as being allowed to invest in mutual funds and corporate bonds, insurance companies should be able to invest in asset management companies and fund management companies. At the same time, in order to improve the solvency of insurance companies, their management mechanisms should be transformed. The emphasis should be placed upon innovation and adjustment of the methods of competition, for example, by strengthening collaboration between Chinese insurance companies so that they can mutually complement each other's advantages, thereby allowing them to compete effectively against the foreign insurance companies. They should be able to develop a level of core competitiveness which their foreign competitors will find it hard to imitate, while at the same time each individual insurance company establishes its own comparative advantage, for example, by improving its traditional insurance products, introducing new products and advanced management techniques from abroad, improving employees service attitude and service skills, and establishing a customer-centered service philosophy. In addition, a collaborative relationship needs to be established between insurance companies and banks so as to create synergy.

In response to China's accession to the WTO, China's life insurance industries have made restructuring, expansion into new business areas and stock market listing their main objectives for 2003. After beginning collaboration with leading international consulting firm Mackenzie in 2002, China Life has redesigned its organizational structure and sales system. In the area of sales management, management is being centralized at the provincial level, with the adoption of an innovative management model which will leverage the company's advantage in terms of the large number of branches. A new risk management mechanism is being adopted based on commercial ceding, and special emphasis is being placed on information system establishment. China Life is also working to optimize its asset structure.

In 2003, China Life will become a share-type company. In 2002, Ping An brought in HSBC as a strategic investor, and established the China Insurance Group; the establishment of separate companies for Ping An's main business areas heralded the emergence of a 'Ping An Financial Holding Company'. Also in 2002, China Pacific implemented a capital increment, bringing about the diversification of its equity structure with the introduction of private investors; China Pacific's capitalization increased to RMB9 billion. China Pacific's strategic goal over the next ten years is, on the basis of the current average annual sales growth of over 55 percent and annual profit growth of over 22 percent, to create an internationalized financial group which will embrace China Pacific's insurance, financial, international and educational businesses. Xin Hua Life Insurance completed a capital increment in 2000; its main goal for 2003 is to complete stock market listing. The People's Insurance Company of China will be making changes to its equity structure in 2003. China Reinsurance will be transformed into a reinsurance group, with the establishment of China Casualty Reinsurance Ltd., China Life Reinsurance Ltd. and China Xin An Casualty Insurance Ltd. The entire equity of the Zhongguo Baoxian Bao Agency, Hua Tai Insurance Brokerage Company and China Insurance Management College (which are all either wholly owned or controlled by China Reinsurance) will be transferred to China Reinsurance (Group). As banks begin to collaborate with securities firms and insurance companies, collaboration is also beginning to take place between securities firms and insurance companies. For example, China Life has signed an agreement with Lianhe Securities to collaborate in all business areas; Xin Hua Life Insurance has formed a strategic alliance with Fujian Development Bank; and Bank of China and China Export Credit Insurance Co. recently signed an agreement in Beijing whereby they will share customer data and collaborate on risk control, new product development, the development of export credit insurance financing guarantee business, e-commerce, settlement, sales and so on.

Establishing a Comprehensive Legal Framework for the Insurance Industry

Now that China is a member of the WTO, the level of competition in the insurance market will grow steadily, ultimately becoming much more intense. However, China's current Insurance Law needs to be revised in line with actual needs. In response to the needs created by WTO accession and the establishment of many new market participants, the Chinese government has already made several revisions to the Insurance Law. These include the abolition of the 20 percent ceding requirement for non-life insurance business, and adjustment of the restrictions imposed on the scope of business of casualty and life insurance companies.

Now the restrictions merely stipulate that no company may engage simultaneously in casualty insurance and life insurance business; both casualty insurance companies and life insurance companies are allowed to sell accident insurance and short-term health insurance. Insurance companies have been given the right to set their own premium rates, with the auditing departments being responsible for review. The prohibitions affecting the employment of insurance company funds have been revised; insurance companies are now allowed to establish securities firms and other types of non-insurance enterprise, and they can use their funds in other types of investment. In addition, supervision of insurance company solvency has been strengthened. For example, insurance company auditing departments are now required to implement monitoring of minimum solvency requirements, and to establish a solvency monitoring system. The regulations governing allocations to liability reserves have been strengthened. Casualty insurance companies are now required to establish actuarial reporting systems, and insurance companies are expected to undertake more effective supervision of agents. A new Insurance Law came into effect on 1 January 2003. The China Insurance Regulatory Commission is also setting to work on the formulation of necessary ancillary legislation, such as the Management Regulations Governing Insurance Brokers.

There is also a need for ancillary legislation such as an Agent Management Law, and Reinsurance Management Law. In the future, foreign insurance companies will no longer be limited to share-type companies and joint venture companies; wholly foreign-owned insurance companies, insurance companies controlled by holding companies and collaborative companies will also appear. Foreign reinsurance companies and intermediary services companies will also be moving into the Chinese market. This means that the Chinese government needs to set about the task of enacting a Statute for the Management of Foreign Insurance Companies as quickly as possible, abolishing the preferential treatment which foreign insurance companies receive, and establishing clear regulations regarding the operations of, and competition among, different types of foreign insurance company.

The Statute for the Management of Foreign Insurance Companies Operating in the People's Republic of China (hereinafter referred to as 'the Statute') came into effect on 1 February 2002. According to the provisions of the Statute, a foreign insurance company wishing to establish itself in China must conform to the following requirements: (i) it must have been in the insurance business for at least thirty years; (ii) it must have had an office in China for at least two years; (iii) in the year prior to the submission of the application, its total assets must not have fallen below US$5 billion; (iv) the country or region in which it operates must have a sound system for the regulation of the insurance industry and the insurance company must already be under the effective supervision of the authorities in the country or region in question; (v) it must conform to the solvency requirements of the country or region in which it operates; (vi) the authorities in the country or region in which it operates must have given their agreement to the application; and (vii) it must conform to all other qualifications imposed by the China Insurance Regulatory Commission.

As far as capitalization is concerned, the Statute stipulates that a joint venture insurance company or wholly foreign-owned insurance company must have capitalization of at least RMB200 million or the equivalent in a freely traded foreign currency, and that this must all be paid-in capital. The capital contribution made by the foreign insurance company must be in a freely traded currency. In the case of a branch of a foreign insurance company, the parent company must allocate to the branch a minimum of RMB200 million or the equivalent in a freely traded foreign currency. In addition, the China Insurance Regulatory Commission may raise the above-mentioned capitalization requirements and the minimum working capital requirements according to the foreign insurance company's business scope and scale of operation.

As regards regulation, the Statute stipulates that the branch of a foreign insurance company must submit its own financial statements and those of the parent company for the previous year to the China Insurance Regulatory Commission within three months of the end of the accounting year, and must make a public announcement of these financial statements. If the parent company of a foreign insurance company branch experiences any change of name, chairman, place of registration or capitalization, or any change in those shareholders holding a share of 10 percent or more of the company's total capital or equity, or if there is any change in the scope of business, or if the company is punished by the regulatory authorities in the country or region in which it operates, or if the company suffers a serious loss, is divided into several different companies, undertakes a merger, is dissolved, has its license revoked or becomes insolvent, the branch must submit a written report to the China Insurance Regulatory Commission as promptly as possible. If the parent company of a foreign insurance company branch is dissolved, has its license revoked or becomes insolvent, the China Insurance Regulatory Commission may prohibit the branch from moving into new business areas. If a foreign insurance company conducts foreign currency insurance business, it must abide by the relevant Chinese regulations governing foreign exchange management. In addition, the Statute stipulates that, except in cases where approval has been obtained from the China Insurance Regulatory Commission, a foreign insurance company may not engage in ceded line transactions, inward reinsurance transactions, the purchase or sale of assets or any other transactions with its affiliates.

Establishing Sound Intermediary Institutions in the Insurance Market

A sound, mature insurance market needs not only sound, mature insurance companies but also a reasonable number of intermediary institutions possessing specialist skills and providing a high standard of service; examples would include insurance agents, insurance brokers and insurance appraisers. This is necessary in order to create a comprehensive insurance service system and reduce operating costs. Now that China has joined the WTO, the key factor for ensuring that Chinese and foreign insurance companies are able to compete on a level playing field is the development of intermediary institutions including agents, brokers, appraisers, and institutions which indirectly provide services to the insurance industry, such as rating agencies, insurance industry associations, accountants, attorneys, auditors, firms of actuaries, and the like. In order to achieve this objective, the government's current policy towards the insurance industry will need to be revised, the regulations governing insurance intermediary institutions will have to be strengthened, the quality of intermediary institutions' manpower will need to be improved, and the government will need to strengthen its regulation of the intermediary institutions.

Establishing an Environment of Fair Competition

The government needs to gradually adjust its tax policy with respect to Chinese and foreign insurance companies, putting an end to the coexistence of two different systems, one for Chinese insurance companies and one for foreign insurance companies. For example, the government should reduce the income tax rate applied to Chinese insurance companies; it should also tax premium income after the deduction of premium-related expenditure and should impose different rates of business tax on different types of insurance business. In this way, the tax burden of Chinese insurance companies can be reduced, thus improving their solvency. In addition, companies should be allowed to list worker group insurance premiums as an operating expense, and individuals' long-term insurance premium expenditure should be tax-deductible. This will help to stimulate the development of the life insurance market in China.

Strengthening the Regulation of the Insurance Industry

In response to the diversification and modernization of foreign insurance companies' operations, China needs to strengthen the regulation of the insurance industry. The government should try to reduce the quantity of administrative review work that needs to be performed, allow premium rates to be set by the market, and gradually change the system of approval regarding premium rates, the establishment of branches, appointments of branch managers, and so on, in order to provide greater flexibility. It should establish an effective monitoring system with respect to insurance companies' disclosure systems, and should encourage self-regulation by insurance industry associations.

At present, however, the Chinese insurance industry's associations are unable to exercise effective supplementary supervision of the insurance market. Insurance companies lack the opportunity to participate in the formulation of standard policy terms and premium rates. Management of professional qualifications, which in other countries is usually handled by the industry association, is still the responsibility of the regulator. As China switches over to a system whereby standard policy terms and premium rates are set by the market, there is a serious lack of underwriting and loss data with respect to different insurance products. In order to avoid a situation where market opening leads to market chaos, it is vital that the industry association step in to undertake centralized collection and collation of data, as well as the design and formulation of standard policy terms and premium rates which can be used as a reference by all insurance companies. The most important task in the process of regulatory innovation is thus how to ensure a proper balance between centralization and decentralization.

As regards having premium rates set by the market, on 1 October 2001 the China Insurance Regulatory Commission gave approval for this to begin on a trial basis with respect to vehicle insurance in Guangdong Province. On 1 January 2003 implementation of a reform of the vehicle insurance policy term and premium rate management system began on a nationwide basis. In order to ensure that both monitoring and handling of violations are undertaken in accordance with the requirements of the law, in July 2001 the Regulations Governing Administrative Review by the China Insurance Industry Regulation and Management Committee were promulgated.

As far as the contents of regulation are concerned, while continuing to regulate premium rates and policy clauses, the government should switch the main focus of regulation over to solvency, strengthen asset and liability monitoring, improve the monitoring infrastructure, and establish mechanisms for bilateral or multilateral exchange and coordination between the regulatory agencies and other government agencies (economic, tax and auditing agencies). There is also a need for closer coordination between the regulatory authorities for the banking industry, insurance industry and securities industry. China can borrow from the experience of other countries, using risk monitoring indicators which focus on solvency as the foundation for establishing an early warning system that conforms to China's own particular needs.

Active Cultivation of Insurance Talent

Since the shortage of personnel with insurance expertise is of major concern within the Chinese insurance industry, the government should aim to promote the cultivation of insurance talent. The insurance industry could, for example, collaborate closely with universities and colleges, making use of their educational resources to cultivate talent and improve the quality of insurance industry manpower. The government also needs to bear in mind that the reinsurance market plays a vital role in spreading risk, ensuring stability and regulating competition. The role played by the reinsurance market is becoming increasingly important throughout the global insurance market; however, China's reinsurance market is still at the very early stages of development and therefore needs to be strengthened considerably in order to meet the challenges of globalization.

As the process of economic globalization has progressed, the economic activities of different countries are gradually becoming interlinked. Any country which hopes to maintain sustainable growth has to exchange material, technology, capital and human resources with other countries. One result of globalization is that different kinds of production factors, and particularly capital, can flow rapidly all over the world. This globalization of the international flow of funds has stimulated competition within the global finance industry, leading to a deepening of financial liberalization in many countries. China, however, lacks a comprehensive, coherent legal framework for the protection of private property rights and regulation of economic activities. As a result, financial reform in China has been slow. It will take time and careful consideration to get right the changes needed to make China's financial system more efficient. The Chinese banking industry and its insurance industry need to speed up the process of reform in line with the needs of globalization, and in response to the new circumstances following China's accession to the WTO.

NOTES

1. For detail discussion, See He (2000), Wang, Yuanlong (2000), Zhou, Qing (2000), Wu, Xiangjiang (2000), Chen Qiuyun (2000), Li and Zhang (2000), Shandong Province Financial Studies Association Project Team (2001), Wang, Shaojin (2001), Tian (2001), Yu, Yuejun (2002), *Zhong Jing Wang* (12 March 2002, 17 May 2002), Xu and Li (2002), *Zhengjuan Ribao* (8 April 2002), *Da Kung Pao* (13 May 2002), *Shichang Bao* (13 May 2002), *Renmin Ribao* (11 April 2002, 24 May 2002), *Guoji Jinrong Bao* (4 April 2002, 7 April 2002, 7 May 2002, 14 May 2002, 27 May 2002, 12 February 2003) and *Zhong Yin Wang* (22 November 2002, 18 December 2002).
2. See Yin (1998), Yuan (1998), Gu (2000), Gao (2000), Liu (2000), Lu (2001), *He Xun Wang* (27 December 2001), *Guoji Jinrong Bao* (24 May 2002, 29 October 2002), Li, Manyun (2002), Meng, Long (2002), *Shichang Bao* (25 April 2002, 28 June 2002), Yu, Jianguang (2002), Zhang, Xiaoqing (2002), *Zhong Xin She* (14 January 2002) and *Zhong Yin Wang* (2 July 2002, 16 December 2002, 24 January 2003, 27 January 2003, 14 February 2003, 17 February 2003).

References

Baoxian Zixun (2000), 'The Global Insurance Market in 1998', *Baoxian Zixun* (*Insurance News*), **176**, 22–43.

Bencivenga, V.R. and B.D. Smith (1991), 'Financial Intermediation and Endogenous Growth', *Review of Economic Studies*, **58** (194), April, 195–209.

Bowles, P. and G. White (1989), 'Contradictions in China's Financial Reforms: The Relationship between Banks and Enterprises', *Cambridge Journal of Economics*, **13** (4), December, 482–95.

Cao, Longqi (2000), 'The Eight Key Issues of Financial Reform in China', *Jinrong yu Baoxian* (*Finance and Insurance*), **6**, 28–34.

Cetorelli, N. and M. Gambera (2001), 'Banking Market Structure, Financial Dependence and Growth: International Evidence from Industry Data', *Journal of Finance*, **56** (2), April, 617–48.

Chen, C.H. (1989), 'Monetary Aggregate and Macroeconomic Performance in Mainland China', *Journal of Comparative Economics*, **13** (2), June, 314–24.

Chen, C.H. (2002), 'Interest Rates, Savings and Income in the Chinese Economy', *Journal of Economic Studies*, **29** (1), June, 59–73.

Chen, Qiuyun (2000), 'WTO Accession – the Chinese Banking Industry's Response Strategy', *Caijin Maoyi* (*Finance & Trade*), **11**, 18–19.

Chen, Wenyu and Haisheng Yin (2001), 'Insurance Appraisers Are an Important Indicator of a Mature Insurance Market', *Jinrong yu Baoxian* (*Finance and Insurance*), **5**, 86–7.

China Daily (2003), 14 January.

China Daily (2003), 23 January.

China Insurance Regulatory Commission (1999–2002), *China Insurance Yearbook*, Beijing: China Insurance Yearbook Editorial Section.

China's Finance and Banking Association (1997–2002), *Almanac of China's Finance and Banking*, Beijing: Almanac of China's Finance and Banking Editorial Section.

Da Kung Pao (2002), 13 May.

Da Kung Pao (2002), 9 November.

Da Kung Pao (2002), 12 November.

Da Kung Pao (2002), 20 November.

Da Peng Securities Project Team (2000), 'The Flow of Commercial Insurance Funds into the Securities Market – Policy and Strategies', *Jinrong yu Baoxian* (*Finance and Insurance*), **2**, 33–42.

Dai, Fengju (2002), 'WTO Accession and the Development of the Insurance Industry in Taiwan, Hong Kong and China', *Baoxian Yanjiu* (*Insurance Studies*), **5**, 4–6.

Demetriades, P.O. and K.A. Hussein (1996), 'Does Financial Development Cause Economic Growth? Time-series Evidence from 16 Countries', *Journal of Development Economics*, **51** (2), December, 387–411.

Deng, Min (2000), 'The History and Future of China's Insurance Industry, Viewed in Terms of Institutional Change', *Jinrong Yanjiu* (*Journal of Financial Research*), **6**, 97–107.

Deng, Shimin (2001), 'Placing Equal Emphasis on Regulation and Support in the Promotion of the Conversion of Commercial Banks to Share-type Banks', *Zhongguo Jinrong* (*China Finance*), **4**, 30–2.

Ding, Mushan and Zhenyu Tang (2000), 'The WTO and the Development of China's Financial Sector', *Jinrong yu Baoxian* (*Finance and Insurance*), **6**, 44–7.

Duan, Ming (2000), 'WTO Accession and Small and Medium-sized Commercial Banks' Response Strategies', *Jinrong Yanjiu* (*Journal of Financial Research*), **2**, 16–19.

Edwards, F.R. (1977), 'Managerial Objectives in Regulated Industries: Expense Preference Behavior in Banking', *Journal of Political Economy*, **85** (1), February, 147–62.

Fan, Hengshan and Linian Guan (1999), *The Chinese Insurance Market* (*Zhongguo Baoxian Shichang*), Hubei: Hubei People's Publishing Company.

Fung, M.K.Y., W.M. Ho and L. Zhu (2000), 'The Impact of Credit Control and Interest Rate Regulation on the Transforming Chinese Economy: An Analysis of Long-run Effects', *Journal of Comparative Economics*, **28** (2), June, 293–320.

Gao, Shutang (2000), 'How China's Domestic Insurance Industry Can Meet the Challenge of WTO Accession', *Jinrong yu Baoxian* (*Finance and Insurance*), **7**, 86–7.

Gilbert, R.A. (1984), 'Bank Market Structure and Competition: A Survey', *Journal of Money, Credit, and Banking*, **16** (4), November, 617–45.

Girardin, E. (1997), *Banking Sector Reform and Credit Control in China*, Paris: OECD.

Gong, Yuchi (2002), 'The Evolution of the Financial System and the Development of New Small and Medium-sized Commercial Banks in China', *Caimo Jingji* (*Finance & Trade Economics*), **2**, 14–17.

Gu, Zufen (2000), 'WTO Accession: Opportunities and Challenges – the Chinese Insurance Industry Faces up to WTO Accession', *Jinrong yu Baoxian* (*Finance and Insurance*), **4**, 105–6.

Guoji Jinrong Bao (2002), 21 February.

Guoji Jinrong Bao (2002), 1 April.

Guoji Jinrong Bao (2002), 4 April.

Guoji Jinrong Bao (2002), 7 April.

Guoji Jinrong Bao (2002), 11 April.

Guoji Jinrong Bao (2002), 7 May.

Guoji Jinrong Bao (2002), 14 May.

Guoji Jinrong Bao (2002), 24 May.

Guoji Jinrong Bao (2002), 27 May.

Guoji Jinrong Bao (2002), 7 June.

Guoji Jinrong Bao (2002), 11 July.

Guoji Jinrong Bao (2002), 29 October.

Guoji Jinrong Bao (2002), 15 November.

Guoji Jinrong Bao (2002), 21 November.

Guoji Jinrong Bao (2002), 12 December.

Guoji Jinrong Bao (2002), 20 December.

Guoji Jinrong Bao (2002), 25 December.

Guoji Jinrong Bao (2003), 12 February.

Hafer, R.W. and A.M. Kutan (1993), 'Further Evidence on Money, Output, and Prices in China', *Journal of Comparative Economics*, **17** (3), September, 701–9.

He, Fang (2000), 'The Merger Fever in the International Banking Industry and What It Means for the Chinese Banking Industry', *Jinrong yu Baoxian* (*Finance and Insurance*), **6**, 48–51.

He Xun Wang http://www.homeway.com.cn/ (2001), 27 December.

He Xun Wang http://www.homeway.com.cn/ (2002), 5 February.

Heggestad, A.A. (1977), 'Market Structure, Risk and Profitability in Commercial Banking', *Journal of Finance*, **32** (4), September, 1207–16.

Hong, Xiaguan (2001), 'Financial Sector Regulation in China Since the Asian Financial Crisis', *Zhongguo Jinrong* (*China Finance*), **9**, 16–18.

Hsiao, K.H.Y. Huang (1982), 'Money and Banking in the People's Republic of China: Recent Developments', *China Quarterly*, **91,** September, 462–77.

Hu, Mingdong and Xiaoxiang Zhao (1998), 'An Analysis of the Unregulated Competition in the Insurance Market and the Development of Regulation', *Jinrong Yanjiu* (*Journal of Financial Research*), **10**, 71–3.

Huang, Jinlao (2000a), 'Creating a Suitable Market Environment for Asset Management Companies', *Zhongguo Jinrong* (*China Finance*), **1**, 24.

Huang, Jinlao (2000b), 'WTO Accession and the Opening up of China's Financial Services Industry', *Jingji Daokan* (*Economic Herald*), **6**, 7–16.

Huang, Jinlao (2002), 'Establishing Sound Corporate Governance Is the Core Element in the Reform of the State-owned Banks', *Jingji Daokan* (*Economic Herald*), **1**, 7–9.

Huang, Liangmou (2001), 'Establishment of an Efficient Mechanism for Bank Regulation under the WTO Framework', *Zhongguo Jinrong* (*China Finance*), **9**, 42–3.

Huang, Min (2000), 'A Comparison of the Transaction Structure of State-owned Banks, and Analysis of Their Risk Status', *Jinrong yu Baoxian* (*Finance and Insurance*), **4**, 50–6.

Huang, Qingming (2002), 'The WTO and the Chinese Insurance Appraisal Industry', *Baoxian Yanjiu* (*Insurance Studies*), **6**, 42–4.

Huang, Zhiling (1992), *Capital Formation and Financial Development* (*Zijin Xingceng yu Jinrong Fazhan*), Beijing: China Finance Publishing Company.

Insurance Industry Development Center (2002), *Development Strategy for the Chinese Insurance Market*, 5 March.

Jiang, Chun, Changsheng Hu, Lei Zhang and Wenxiang Wang (2001), *How the Chinese Financial Sector Can Respond Successfully to WTO Accession* (*Zhongguo Jinrongye Cengknog Endui WTO*), Wuchang: Wuhan University Press.

Jiang, Minsheng (2002), 'The Operational Status of Asset Management Companies and the Clearing up of Non-performing Loans', *Zhongguo Jinrong* (*China Finance*), **1**, 25–6.

Jiao, Jinpu (2000), *The WTO and the Future of China's Financial Industry* (*WTO yu Zhongguo Jinrong Weilai*), Beijing: Zhongguo Jinrong Press.

Jiao, Jinpu (2002), 'Business Systems and Business Innovation in China's Commercial Banks', *Jingji Daokan* (*Economic Herald*), **1**, 55–9.

Jingji Daobao (*Economic Reporter*) (2002), **2754**, 14 January.

Jingji Ribao (2002), 15 January.

Jinrong Shibao (2002), 31 January.

Kornai, J. (1980), *Economics of Shortage*, Amsterdam: North-Holland Publishing Company.

Leung, C.K.Y. (2001), 'Productivity Growth, Increasing Income Inequality and Social Insurance: The Case of China?', *Journal of Economic Behavior & Organization*, **46** (4), December, 395–408.

Leung, M.K, D. Rigby and T. Young (2003), 'Entry of Foreign Banks in the People's Republic of China: A Survival Analysis', *Applied Economics*, **35** (1), January, 21–31.

Levine, R. (1997), 'Financial Development and Economic Growth: View and Agenda', *Journal of Economic Literature*, **35** (2), June, 688–726.

Levine, R. and S. Zervos (1998), 'Stock Markets, Banks, and Economic Growth', *American Economic Review*, **88** (3), June, 537–58.

Levine, R., N. Loayza, and T. Beck (2000), 'Financial Intermediation and Growth: Causality and Causes', *Journal of Monetary Economics*, **46** (1), August, 31–77.

Li, Guofeng (2001), 'Systemic Innovation in State-owned Commercial Banks', *Zhongnan Caijing Zhengfa Daxue Xuebao* (*Journal of Zhongnan University of Economics and Law*), **6**, 96–9.

Li, Hongyan (2001), 'Basic Problems Relating to Policy Finance', *Juece Jiejian* (*Policy Making Reference*), **6**, 14–18.

Li, Kaifu and Hualin Wei (2001), 'International Comparison of Insurance Industry Policy and the Lessons It Offers', *Jingji Pinlun* (*Economic Review*), **6**, 82–90.

Li, Kunhong (1999), 'Adjustment of Insurance Company Management Strategies in an Era of Low Growth', *Baoxian Yanjiu* (*Insurance Studies*), **7**, 9–11.

Li, Manyun (2002), 'Seizing Opportunities to Further the Development of the Chinese Insurance Industry', *Jinrong yu Baoxian* (*Finance and Insurance*), **3**, 145–9.

Li, Sen and Yong Zhang (2000), 'WTO Accession and China's State-owned Commercial Banks', *Touzi Yanjiu* (*Investment Research*), **11**, 20–3.

Li, X. and Y. Ma (1996), 'Financial Reforms and Regional Investment Conflicts in China: A Game-theoretic Analysis', *Economics of Planning*, **29** (2), 117–30.

Li, Xuan and Yan Li (2001), 'The New Round of Financial Reform in China Following the Asian Financial Crisis', *Zhongguo Jinrong* (*China Finance*), **2**, 32–4.

Li, Yousheng (1998), *Good News or Bad News? Problems Affecting the Chinese Insurance Industry* (*Huoxi? Fuxi? Zhongguo Baoxianye Wenti Baogao*), Shenyang: Shenyang Publishing Company.

Lin, C.Z. (1995), 'The Assessment: Chinese Economic Reform in Retrospect and Prospect', *Oxford Review of Economic Policy*, **11** (4), Winter, 1–24.

Lin, Yifu (2000), 'State-owned Investment Companies and the Marketization of State-owned Capital', China Economic Research Center, Beijing University, November.

Liu, Cheng (2000), 'The Chinese Insurance Industry and International Competition', *Jinrong yu Baoxian* (*Finance and Insurance*), **7**, 88–9.

Liu, Chongming and Panwen Wu (2000), 'WTO Accession, the Challenges Faced by the Banking Industry in Tianjin, and Response Strategies', *Jinrong Yanjiu* (*Journal of Financial Research*), **12**, 86–91.

Liu, Fei (2001), 'The Utilization of Insurance Company Funds in China – Problems and Response Strategies', *Jingji Daokan* (*Economic Herald*), **6**, 55–8.

Liu, G.G., X. Wu, C. Peng and A.Z. Fu (2003), 'Urbanization and Health Care in Rural China', *Contemporary Economic Policy*, **21** (14), January, 11–24.

Liu, Jin (2001), 'Reflections on the Stock Market Listing of Banks in China', *Jingji yu Guanli Yanjiu* (*Economic and Management Studies*), **1**, 62–4.

Liu, Jinglun (2002), 'Market Entity Cultivation in China Following WTO Accession', *Baoxian Yanjiu* (*Insurance Studies*), **1**, 8–10.

Liu, Xiaomei and Qiang Chen (2000), 'Analysis of Trends in the Chinese Insurance Market in 2000', *Jinrong yu Baoxian* (*Finance and Insurance*), **7**, 92–5.

Liu, Xiliang and Dezhi Luo (2001), 'The Sources of Non-performing Assets in China's Banking Industry', *Jinrong Yanjiu* (*Journal of Financial Research*), **10**, 50–9.

Lu, Anping (1998), 'Thoughts on Insurance Fund Utilization', *Jinrong Yanjiu* (*Journal of Financial Research*), **7**, 64–6.

Lu, Yu (2001), 'Various Problems Relating to the Development of the Chinese Insurance Industry', *Zhongguo Jinrong* (*China Finance*), **4**, 45–6.

Luan, Cuncun (1998), 'New Thinking Regarding the Investment of Insurance Company Funds in China', *Caijing Yanjiu* (*The Study of Finance and Economics*), **10**, 27–30.

Lucas, R.E. (1988), 'On the Mechanics of Economic Development', *Journal of Monetary Economics*, **22** (1), July, 3–42.

Ma, J. (1995), 'China: Central Government Credibility and Economic Overheating', *Economic Systems*, **19** (3) , September, 237–61.

McKinnon, R.I. (1973), *Money and Capital in Economic Development*, Washington, DC: Brookings Institution.

Meng, Long (2002), 'The Impact of WTO Accession on the Regulation of the Chinese Insurance Industry', *Baoxian Yanjiu* (*Insurance Studies*), **2**, 14–15.

Pan, Shujuan (2001), 'Human Resources Development: The Banking Industry's Choices with Respect to Stemming the Outward Flow of Talent', *Jingji Wenti* (*On Economic Problems*), **5**, 54–7.

Park, A. and K. Sehrt (2001), 'Tests of Financial Intermediation and Banking Reform in China', *Journal of Comparative Economics*, **29** (4), December, 608–44.

Peng, Xuemei (2000), 'The Selection of Regulatory Models for China's Insurance Industry', *Jinrong Yanjiu* (*Journal of Financial Research*), **1**, 121–8.

People's Bank of China Tax Survey Team (2000), 'Survey into the Fees Handled by Chinese Banks', *Jinrong Yanjiu* (*Journal of Financial Research*), **11**, 67–77.

Qin, Wanshun and Jun Ouyang (2002), 'Expense Preference and Scale Preference Behavior in China's Wholly State-owned Commercial Banks', *Jinrong Yanjiu* (*Journal of Financial Research*), **1**, 63–74.

Qu, Hong, Mingming Wang and Zhixiang Yang (2001), 'Disclosure of Risk in Listed Chinese Commercial Banks – Theory and Empirical Research', *Guanli Shijue* (*Management World)*, **1**, 132–7.

Rajan, R.G. and L. Zingales (1998), 'Financial Dependence and Growth', *American Economic Review*, **88** (3), June, 559–86.

Renmin Ribao (*People's Daily*) (2002), 11 April.

Renmin Ribao (*People's Daily*) (2002), 24 May.

Renmin Ribao (*People's Daily*) (2002), 13 July.

Renmin Ribao (*People's Daily*) (2002), 4 November.

Robinson, J. (1952), 'The Generalization of the General Theory', in *The Rate of Interest, and Other Essays*, London: Macmillan, 67–142.

Saint-Paul, G. (1992), 'Technological Choice, Financial Markets and Economic Development', *European Economic Review*, **36** (4), May, 763–81.

Scherer, F.M. (1980), *Industrial Market Structure and Economics Performance*, Chicago: Rand McNally College Publishing Company.

Schumpeter, J.A. (1934), *The Theory of Economic Development*, Cambridge, MA: Harvard University Press.

Shandong Province Financial Studies Association Project Team (2001), 'WTO Accession and the Development Strategy of Chinese Commercial Banks', *Jinrong Yanjiu* (*Journal of Financial Research*), **2**, 115–22.

Shaw, E.S. (1973), *Financial Deepening in Economic Development*, New York: Oxford University Press.
Shen, Shuguang (2000), *Insurance Regulation* (*Baoxian Jianguan*), Guangzhou: Zhongshan University Press.
Sheng, Liurong (2001), 'Comparison of the Strengths and Weaknesses of State-owned Commercial Banks and Foreign Commercial Banks', *Touzi Yanjiu* (*Investment Research*), **3**, 2–6.
Shi, Wenqing (1999), *The Regulation of the Commercial Insurance Business in China* (*Zhingguo Shangye Baoxian Jiandu Guanli Wenti*), Beijing: Jingji Kexue Press.
Shichang Bao (2002), 24 January.
Shichang Bao (2002), 25 April.
Shichang Bao (2002), 13 May.
Shichang Bao (2002), 28 June.
Shichang Bao (2002), 16 July.
Shichang Bao (2002), 11 December.
Shichang Bao (2002), 17 December.
Shichang Bao (2002), 19 December.
Smirlock, M. (1985), 'Evidence on the (Non) Relationship between Concentration and Profitability in Banking', *Journal of Money, Credit, and Banking*, **17** (1), February, 69–83.
Song, Qinghua (2001), 'Banking Crisis: China Needs to Face up to Reality', *Jinrong yu Baoxian* (*Finance and Insurance*), **2**, 48–52.
Sun, Bing (2002), 'The Challenges Facing China's Insurance Market', *Baoxian Yanjiu* (*Insurance Studies*), **2**, 25.
Ta Kung Pao (2002), 6 February.
Tan, Qilian and Xinghua Gao (2001), 'The Reasons for the Disparity Between the Potential Market for Non-life Insurance in China and the Actual Market Size', *Jinrong yu Baoxian* (*Finance and Insurance*), **1**, 119–24.
Tian, Dongwen (2001), 'The Opening up of the Chinese Banking Industry and the Adjustment of the Relevant Laws and Regulations', *Guoji Jingji Hezuo* (*International Economic Cooperation*), **12**, 11–14.
Wang, Anran (2002), 'China's Insurance Intermediary Industry', *Baoxian Yanjiu* (*Insurance Studies*), **6**, 28–9.
Wang, Chunhan (2000), 'The Market Positioning of China's Small and Medium-sized Commercial Banks Following WTO Accession', *Jinrong Yanjiu* (*Journal of Financial Research*), **8**, 104–7.
Wang, Fang (2002), 'The WTO and the Development of China's Re-insurance Market', *Jinrong yu Baoxian* (*Finance and Insurance*), **5**, 134–5.
Wang, Ping (2001), 'Several Issues Regarding the Utilization of Insurance Funds in China', *Zhongguo Jinrong* (*China Finance*), **9**, 46–7.
Wang, Shaojin (2001), 'The Prospects for Cross-industry Operation in China's Financial Sector', *Shangye Yanjiu* (*Commercial Research*), **12**, 83–4.
Wang, Wenxiang and Hualin Wei (2002), 'Policy Adjustment to Enhance Innovation and Improve the Competitiveness of Chinese Insurance Companies', *Baoxian Yanjiu* (*Insurance Studies*), **11**, 6–10.
Wang, Xingyi (2000), 'Asset Management Company Operation and Risk Management', *Zhongguo Jinrong* (*China Finance*), **12**, 8–10.
Wang, Yuanlong (2000), 'The Development of the Chinese Banking Industry Following WTO Accession', *Jinrong Yanjiu* (*Journal of Financial Research*), **3**, 37–46.

Wang, Zhenshan (2000), 'Bank Size and the Operational Performance of China's Commercial Banks', *Caimo Jingji* (*Finance & Trade Economics*), **5**, 19–22.

Wang, Zili (2001), 'The Feasibility of Capital Increments by the Wholly State-owned Commercial Banks', *Jinrong Yanjiu* (*Journal of Financial Research*), **11**, 1–10.

Wei, S.J. and T. Wang (1997), 'The Siamese Twins: Do State-owned Banks Favor State-owned Enterprises in China?', *China Economic Review*, **8** (1), Spring, 19–29.

Wei, Yu and Li Wang (2000), 'The Efficiency of China's Commercial Banks – A Non-parameter Analysis', *Jinrong Yanjiu* (*Journal of Financial Research*), **3**, 88–96.

Williamson, O.E. (1963), 'Managerial Discretion and Business Behavior', *American Economic Review*, **53** (5), December, 1032–57.

Wu, Peng (2001), 'The Prospects for Group Insurance Business Following WTO Accession', *Baoxian Yanjiu* (*Insurance Studies*), **10**, 22–4.

Wu, Xiangjiang (2000), 'WTO Accession and Financial Innovation in China's Commercial Banks', *Caijing Wenti Yanjiu* (*Research on Financial and Economic Issues*), **9**, 26–9.

Wu, Yue (2000), 'The Preliminary Work in the Establishment of a Financial Asset Management System Has Been Completed', *Zhongguo Jinrong* (*China Finance*), **1**, 23.

Xinhua News Agency (2002), 5 December.

Xu, Fangming and Hanling Li (2002), 'WTO Accession and Financial Deregulation in China', *Caimo Jingji* (*Finance & Trade Economics*), **2**, 31–4.

Xu, Xuemin (2000), 'Banks During the Period of Transformation – Restructuring of Corporate Relationships', *Caimo Jingji* (*Finance & Trade Economics*), **2**, 40–3.

Yang, Fan (2000), 'Analysis of Sunrise Industries of the 21st Century: The Chinese Insurance Industry – Current Status and Future Prospects', *Jinrong yu Baoxian* (*Finance and Insurance*), **2**, 43–4.

Yang, Tao (2000), 'The Problems Faced by the Policy Banks, and Their WTO Accession Response Strategies', *Caijing Kexue* (*Finance and Economics*), **6**, 25–9.

Yao, Qinghai (2000), 'Cultivating the Insurance Intermediary Market to Strengthen the Structure of the Chinese Insurance Market', *Zhongguo Jinrong* (*China Finance*), **6**, 42–3.

Yao, Shixin (2001), 'Which Insurance Company Has the Highest Reputation?', *Jinrong yu Baoxian* (*Finance and Insurance*), **2**, 143–4.

Yin, Shuhao (1998), 'The Development of China's Insurance Market', *Xiandai Caijing* (*Modern Finance*), **6**, 48–50.

Yu, Jianguang (2002), 'The Development of the Chinese Insurance Industry and Industry Regulation', *Baoxian Yanjiu* (*Insurance Studies*), **1**, 28–9.

Yu, Q. (1997), 'Economic Fluctuation, Macro Control, and Monetary Policy in the Transitional Chinese Economy', *Journal of Comparative Economics*, **25** (2), October, 180–95.

Yu, Yuejun (2002), "The Impact of Foreign Shareholding On the Financial Industry's Regulatory System", in *Jingji Cankao Bao*, http://www.cfn.com.cn/, 15 November.

Yuan, Huajun, Li Da and Xinru Tian (2000), 'The Regulation of Foreign Banks Following WTO Accession – Challenges and Responses', *Jinrong yu Baoxian* (*Finance and Insurance*), **10**, 69–73.

Yuan, Li (1998), 'A Preliminary Exploration of Insurance Industry Regulation in China', *Baoxian Yanjiu* (*Insurance Studies*), **11**, 6–8.

Yusuf, S. (1994), 'China's Macroeconomic Performance and Management during Transition', *Journal of Economic Perspectives*, **8** (2), Spring, 71–92.

Zhang, Biao (2000), 'Systemic Innovation in the State-owned Commercial Banks and Overall Financial Sector Supervision', *Caimo Jingji* (*Finance & Trade Economics*), **12**, 31–4.

Zhang, Xiaoqing (2002), 'The Chinese Insurance Industry's Development Strategy in the Face of International Competition', *Jinrong yu Baoxian* (*Finance and Insurance*), **5**, 131–3.

Zhang, Zhaojie and Yanhua Zhang (2002), 'Moving Out of the Grey Zone – Conventional and Unconventional Response Strategies for State-owned Banks Faced with the Entry of Foreign Banks into the Market', *Guoji Maoyi* (*Intertrade*), **4**, 49–53.

Zheng, Jianghuai and Yuze Gao (2000), 'Financial Development in China and Bank Performance', *Jingji Lilun yu Jingji Guanli* (*Economic Theory and Business Management*), **6**, 19–24.

Zhengjuan Ribao (2002), 25 February.

Zhengjuan Ribao (2002), 8 April.

Zhengjuan Shibao (*Securities Times*) (2003), 23 January.

Zhong Jing Wang http://www.cei.gov.cn/ (2002), 12 March.

Zhong Jing Wang http://www.cei.gov.cn/ (2002), 17 May.

Zhong, Wei (2001), 'China's WTO Accession and Bank Development Strategy', *Touzi Yanjiu* (*Investment Research*), **2**, 13–17.

Zhong Xin She (2002), 14 January.

Zhong Yin Wang http://www.cfn.com.cn/ (2001), 'The Preliminary Formation of a Four-in-one Insurance Regulation System', 29 November.

Zhong Yin Wang http://www.cfn.com.cn/ (2002), 2 July.

Zhong Yin Wang http://www.cfn.com.cn/ (2002), 3 July.

Zhong Yin Wang http://www.cfn.com.cn/ (2002), 'The Comparative Advantage of China's Small and Medium-sized Commercial Banks Following WTO Accession', 30 September.

Zhong Yin Wang http://www.cfn.com.cn/ (2002), 'New Developments in China's Banking Industry Following WTO Accession', 22 November.

Zhong Yin Wang http://www.cfn.com.cn/ (2002), 'WTO Accession Has Not Destroyed the Chinese Insurance Industry', 16 December.

Zhong Yin Wang http://www.cfn.com.cn/ (2002), 'SWOT Analysis of the Impact of WTO Accession on Competition between China's Commercial Banks', 18 December.

Zhong Yin Wang http://www.cfn.com.cn/ (2002), 'Inter-bank Business Following WTO Accession – Perspectives and Response Strategies', 23 December.

Zhong Yin Wang http://www.cfn.com.cn/ (2003), 'The Insurance Industry Is Changing Even Faster Than Originally Planned', 14 January.

Zhong Yin Wang http://www.cfn.com.cn/ (2003), 'Entry into and Withdrawal from the Chinese Insurance Market by Foreign Insurance Companies', 22 January.

Zhong Yin Wang http://www.cfn.com.cn/ (2003), 'The Prospects for the Chinese Insurance Industry', 22 January.

Zhong Yin Wang http://www.cfn.com.cn/ (2003), '2003 Will See A Lot of Restructuring by Insurance Companies', 24 January.

Zhong Yin Wang http://www.cfn.com.cn/ (2003), 'The Insurance Industry Faces Major Challenges as It Struggles to Innovate', 27 January.

Zhong Yin Wang http://www.cfn.com.cn/ (2003), 'Last Year, the Chinese Reinsurance Industry Had Total Premium Income of RMB19.178 Billion', 13 February.

Zhong Yin Wang http://www.cfn.com.cn/ (2003), 'The Three Major Problems Affecting the Chinese Reinsurance Industry', 14 February.

Zhong Yin Wang http://www.cfn.com.cn/ (2003), 'Foreign Companies Are Already Moving into the Insurance Intermediary Market', 17 February.

Zhongguo Zhengjuanbao (2003), 21 February.

Zhongguo Zixun Bao (2003), 8 February.

Zhonghua Gongshang Shibao (2002), 25 April.

Zhou, Jiansong (2000), 'The Adjustment and Development of China's Commercial Banking System', *Jinrong Yanjiu* (*Journal of Financial Research*), **12**, 122–5.

Zhou, Qing (2000), 'The Impact of WTO Accession on China's Commercial Banking Industry, and the Response Strategies', *Jinrong yu Baoxian* (*Finance and Insurance*), **10**, 42–4.

Zhou, X. and L. Zhu (1987), 'China's Banking System: Current Status, Perspective on Reform', *Journal of Comparative Economics*, **11** (3), September, 399–409.

Zhu, Junsheng, Ruizong Qi and Guozhu Tuo (2001), 'The Time Is Right for the Marketization of Insurance Premium Rates', *Baoxian Yanjiu* (*Insurance Studies*), **7**, 26–8.

Index